A MATHEMATICAL PANDORA'S BOX

Brian Bolt

CAMBRIDGE
UNIVERSITY PRESS

Published by the Press Syndicate of the University of Cambridge
The Pitt Building, Trumpington Street, Cambridge CB2 1RP
40 West 20th Street, New York, NY 10011-4211, USA
10 Stamford Road, Oakleigh, Melbourne 3166, Australia

First published 1993

Printed in Great Britain by Scotprint, Musselburgh, Scotland

A catalogue record for this book is available from the British Library

Library of Congress cataloguing in publication data
Bolt, Brian.
A mathematical Pandora's box / Brian Bolt.
      p.   cm.
ISBN 0 521 44619 8 (pbk.)
1. Mathematical recreations.   I. Title.
QA95.B57   1993
793.7′4–dc20   92–45680   CIP

ISBN 0 521 44619 8

Cover illustration by Tony Hall
Text cartoons by Harry Venning

Also by this author

Mathematical Activities
More Mathematical Activities
Even More Mathematical Activities
Mathematics Meets Technology
101 Mathematical Projects (with David Hobbs)

VN

CONTENTS

Page numbers in **bold** refer to the activities,
the second page number to the commentary.

Introduction

This is the fourth in my series of mathematical puzzle books. But this last is something of a misnomer for they contain, in addition to many puzzles, a mix of mathematical games, tricks, models to make, and explanations of interesting ideas and phenomena.

The collection put together here contains, in all, 142 new items gleaned from many sources. Some of the ideas are hundreds of years old while others are entirely original and published here for the first time. Just before starting this book I was privileged to lecture at a conference of mathematics teachers in Japan, and the ongoing correspondence this has generated reinforces my belief in the world-wide interest in the kind of activities included here. They not only stimulate creative thinking, but make the reader aware of areas of mathematics in which they might otherwise be quite ignorant. The experienced mathematician will often be aware of the underlying theory which is the basis of a puzzle, but its solution does not normally require any great mathematical knowledge; rather it requires mathematical insight and tenacity. The ability to persist, to reflect, to research, and to call on other experiences is the key to a successful conclusion. When all else fails there is the detailed, but essential, commentary at the end of the book which will often add more insight even when you have found a solution, and will sometimes offer a follow-up problem.

I never cease to be amazed at the variety of interesting puzzles which can arise just from a squared board and a set of counters or coins, and I have spent many enjoyable hours sorting out the solutions to the ones included here. It was interesting for me to learn that even such noteworthy setters of puzzles as Henry Dudeney would sometimes make mistakes in their solutions. None of my solutions are knowingly incorrect, but there may well be better ones, and I would be glad to hear from you if you find one.

Special thanks are due for the ideas and encouragement received from Professor Roger Eggleton, Yoshio Kimura, Irene Domingo, Tim Brierley, Joe Gilks, John Costello, and Susan Gardner of Cambridge University Press.

1 A fabulous family!

Great Grandmother Bountiful, who only had daughters, realised that each of them had produced as many sons as they had sisters, and no daughters. In turn, each of her grandsons had produced as many daughters as he had brothers. She was delighted to recount this to her friends and, furthermore, that the total number of her daughters, grandsons and great-granddaughters was the same as her age!

How old was she?

2 Damage limitation!

Fateful Fred had lost all his money betting on the horses, but he still owned a gold chain with seven links, which a friendly jeweller agreed to value at £20 a link. The result was that Fred bet £20 on each of the next seven horse races, settling his debts at the betting shop after each race by a visit to the jeweller to sell another link, for, as you might have guessed, he kept on losing!

What was the smallest number of links of the chain the jeweller would need to cut so that Fred could meet his outstanding debts after each race?

9

3 Primeval instincts!

In the accompanying sum, different letters represent different digits. Find a solution.

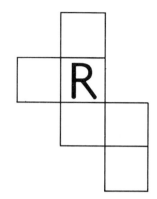

```
  CATS
+ HATE
------
 DOGS
```

4 Spatial perception

Three views of the same cube which has a letter on each of its faces are shown. Also given is a net for the cube but with only one of the letters marked on it. The challenge is to mark in all the other letters, getting their positions and their orientations correct, without resorting to the use of a model cube.

How good is your three-dimensional perception?

5 Spawning coins!

Arrange twelve coins to form a square as shown. Now rearrange them to leave the square intact, but so that each side contains five coins instead of four.

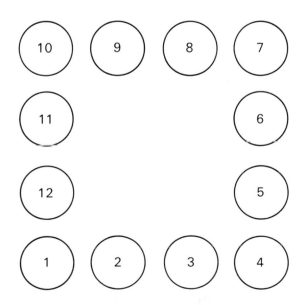

6 Think again!

Can a fraction whose numerator is less than its denominator be equal to a fraction whose numerator is greater than its denominator?

7 Matchstick machinations!

In each of the arrangements of matchsticks, change the position of, but do not remove, four matches to make an arrangement of three squares.

(a)

(b)

(c)

8 Keep off my line!

A board is marked out with a 6 × 6 array of dots joined by a pattern of lines as shown. What is the largest number of counters (or coins) which can be placed on the dots so that no two of them lie on the same line?

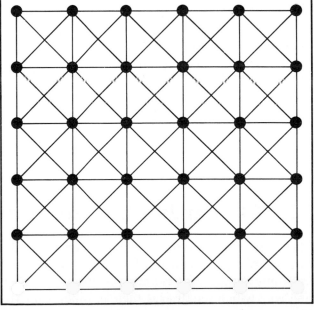

9 Printing the parish magazine

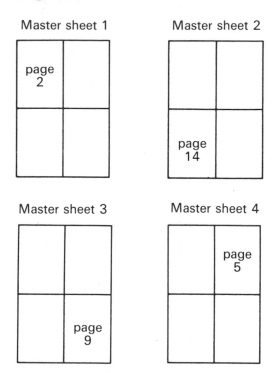

Master sheet 1 — page 2

Master sheet 2 — page 14

Master sheet 3 — page 9

Master sheet 4 — page 5

Mrs Goodbody was the editor of the parish magazine. Each month she produced an A5 size, sixteen-page magazine by first typing the pages separately, and then pasting them, four at a time, onto four A3 master sheets. These were then photocopied, back to back, on A3 paper before she cut the paper in half horizontally and assembled the sheets in the correct order, stapling them down the middle and finally folding them along the line of the staples.

Unfortunately, one month Mrs Goodbody was in a flap, for she had lost the blueprint which told her in which order to paste the typewritten pages onto the master sheets. She was sure of the position of only four of the pages, those indicated on the figure. Where should the other pages go?

10 Maximise the product

There are many ways in which the digits 1, 2, 3, 4, . . . 9 can be arranged to form a four-digit number and a five-digit number, for example 5324 and 89716, but only one way which maximises their product. Can you find it?

11 Honey bears' picnic!

The three bears knew their luck was in when they stumbled across an unopened jar filled to the brim with 21 fluid ounces of delicious golden honey in an abandoned fur-trapper's hut. Wanting to avoid a squabble among themselves, they searched around for some means by which they could share out their spoil fairly. Eventually they found three containers with capacities of 11, 8 and 5 fluid ounces respectively, and set about distributing the honey so that they would each have 7 fluid ounces. They almost gave up in frustration but, being intelligent bears, they persisted until they had solved their distribution problem.

Would you have succeeded?

12 Can you do better?

Six numbers have been cleverly chosen and arranged in the segments of a five-spoked wheel, with its central hub, so that the number in a segment, or the total of the numbers in a set of adjoining segments, can give all the numbers from 1 to 35. For example, $26 = 18 + 6 + 1 + 1$.

Fit the numbers 1, 2, 4, 6, 6, 20 into a similar wheel so that all the numbers from 1 to 39 are obtainable.

Now you appreciate the problem, see how much better you can do with your own choice of numbers for the segments.

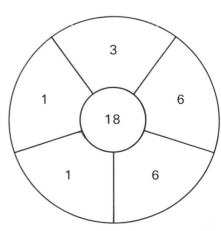

13 The Soma cube

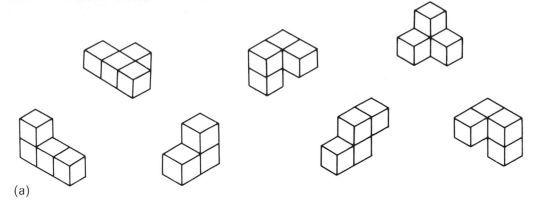

(a)

The Danish mathematician Piet Hein, the creator of this puzzle, little knew the many thousands of hours which would be spent by countless people around the world trying to fit the seven pieces shown in figure (a) into a $3 \times 3 \times 3$ cube. These pieces are often to be found as a commercial puzzle made from plastic, but a more satisfying set can easily be made from wood, and give you hours of amusement.

Start by buying a length of wood with a 2 cm by 2 cm cross-section and then cut off suitable lengths to stick together to form the pieces. For example, the first two shapes are each formed by cutting off a 6 cm length and a 2 cm length.

When you have your set, first try forming the cube (the solution is not unique) and then try using all the pieces to make the shapes shown in figure (b).

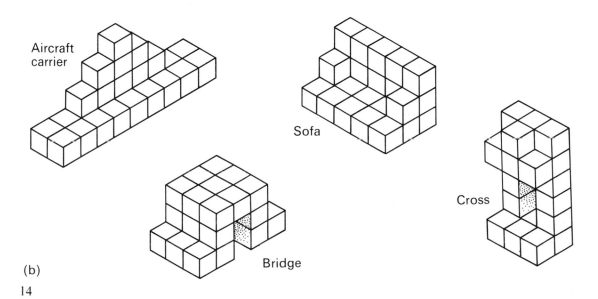

Aircraft carrier

Sofa

Cross

Bridge

(b)

14   Arboreal alignments!

To make the most of the available space, Lady Beechwood wanted to plant her trees in as imaginative a way as possible. In one corner of her park she had her gardeners plant 11 redwood trees so that they formed six rows with four in each row. But her *pièce de résistance*, her centre-piece, was an arrangement of 19 copper-beeches which formed nine rows with five trees in each row.

How did she achieve these feats?

15   Telaga Buruk

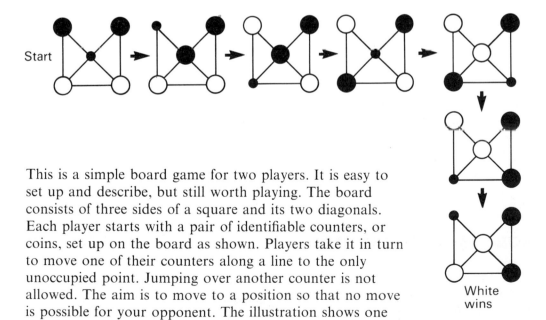

This is a simple board game for two players. It is easy to set up and describe, but still worth playing. The board consists of three sides of a square and its two diagonals. Each player starts with a pair of identifiable counters, or coins, set up on the board as shown. Players take it in turn to move one of their counters along a line to the only unoccupied point. Jumping over another counter is not allowed. The aim is to move to a position so that no move is possible for your opponent. The illustration shows one possible sequence of moves, where black starts but white wins.

16　The Japanese water garden

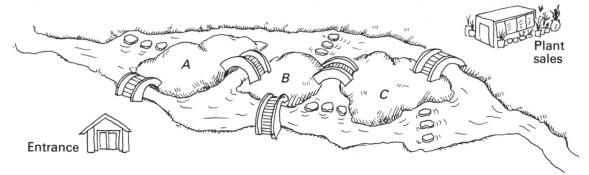

A Japanese water garden had been designed by damming a stream to form a large lake, creating three islands and building a number of bridges and stepping stones connecting them as shown. The garden was very popular with the public, who flocked to see it in large numbers, particularly at holiday times. The result was that the narrow bridges became very congested and the visitors disillusioned at having to queue to cross them.

The head gardener decided that, to avoid the confusion, he would need to devise a route so that having entered at the south bank the visitors would cross the bridges and stepping stones in a predetermined order, crossing each one once, and ending up at the plant sales area before leaving. However, try as he could, he seemed unable to find such a route. But his young assistant, Bridget Oiler, soon saw how to solve the problem by building another bridge.

Where would she build it?

17　Mental gymnastics!

$$GO \times SIX = UP \times TEN$$

Each letter stands for a different digit but, to avoid confusion, O is zero, so now it's over to you!

18　An isosceles dissection

Find a way of cutting up the regular pentagon into four isosceles triangles which can be rearranged to form the symmetric trapezium shown.

16

19 Domino magic

Use eighteen of the dominoes from a standard double-six set to form a 6 × 6 square in such a way that the number of dots in each of the six rows and columns and the two main diagonals is the same.

20 The meal track

A spider is in the top corner *A* of a rectangular room, 20 ft long, 15 ft wide and 10 ft high. It spots a tasty meal in the furthest corner of the room at *G*. What is the shortest distance the spider could travel along the surfaces of the room to claim its prize?

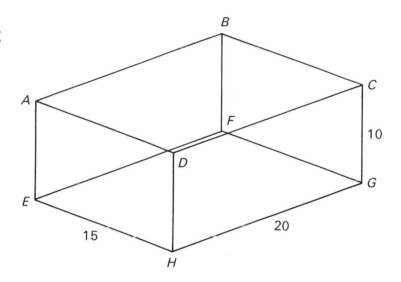

21 The time trial

A 20-mile time trial was held on a straight stretch of road along a river valley, with the cyclists travelling in one direction for 10 miles, turning around, and then retracing their route to the start. Jonathan was up early, very keen to equal the course record which was equivalent to an average speed of 30 mph. Unfortunately, there was a very strong head wind on the outward journey so he only averaged 15 mph to the turn. At what speed must he cycle back, with the following wind to help him, if he is to achieve his objective?

22 Together in threes

CAR	STEM	BOIL
IRENE	WEB	ROWS
TAIL	KNOT	BANK

These nine words have been arranged, at random, in a
3 × 3 array. What is the smallest number of words you
would need to move to rearrange them into a 3 × 3 array
so that the three words in each row, column and diagonal
have a letter in common?

23 Symmetric years

1991 was a beautiful year for not only is it symmetric, but
its prime factors are also all symmetric:

$$1991 = 11 \times 181$$

We call this fully symmetric.

For which years has this been true since the year 1000?

How often will it happen again before we reach the year
3000?

24 A circuitous guard inspection

The palace of a notorious
dictator is surrounded by the
network of roads shown in
the accompanying map. At
each of the lettered junctions
there is a guard post, and it is
the responsibility of the
officer on duty, who is based
at *A*, to inspect every one of
them each hour and return to
base. Can you find a way
which would enable him to
visit each post once only on
his rounds?

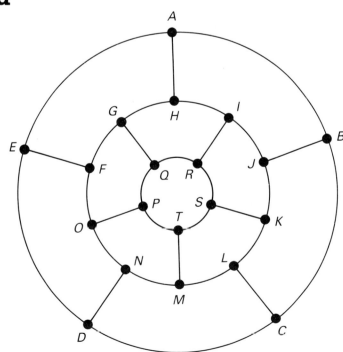

25 Crossing the lakes

Ambuj and Bob and their wives Charulata and Debbie are on an expedition in Alaska which often requires that they cross a lake in their inflatable boat. The boat can carry a maximum load of 100 kg, which is the weight of each of the husbands. The wives, who each weigh 50 kg, carry the boat between them across country while their husbands each carry a rucksack weighing 25 kg. How can they safely negotiate each lake they meet on their expedition without getting wet, assuming they can all paddle the boat if required?

26 Know the time!

It takes only a few seconds' reflection to appreciate that once every hour the minute hand and the hour hand must point in precisely opposite directions. But how often in a day will each hand be pointing exactly at a minute division at the same time as the hands are precisely opposite each other?

27 Half a cube

The six drawings show
different ways of dividing a
cube into identical halves.
There is no end to the
number of ways of doing this.

It is great fun finding your
own particular versions of
half a cube, and then making
models of them, using card or
wood, that fit neatly together.

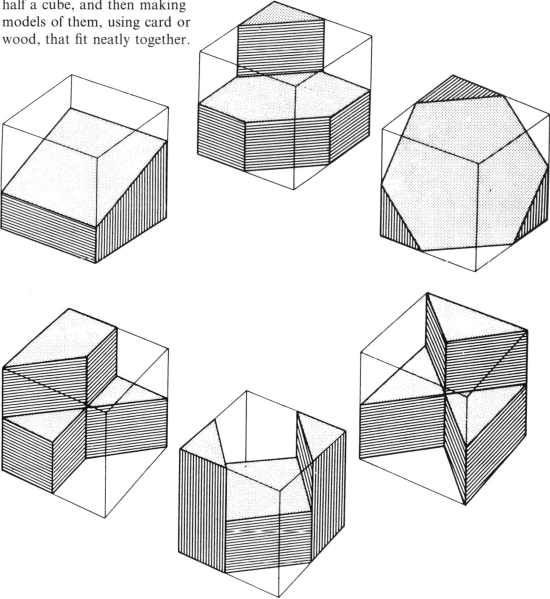

28 Pinball pursuits

Find a route on each of these circular pinball games to
maximise your score. Starting at S, you may move one
square at a time to the right or left or up or down. No
square can be entered if it has a pin in it or if it has already
been visited. You can finish anywhere. Add up the numbers
in the squares you visit and find a route to give you the
biggest possible total. One route is shown in the first game
which has a total of 440, but it can be bettered!

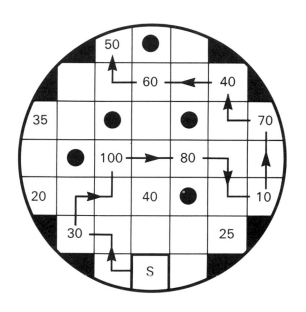

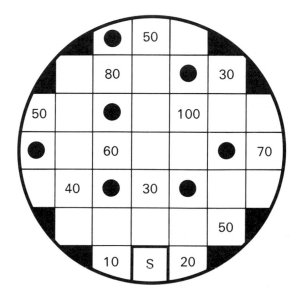

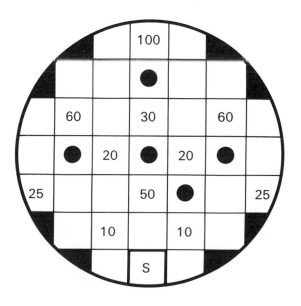

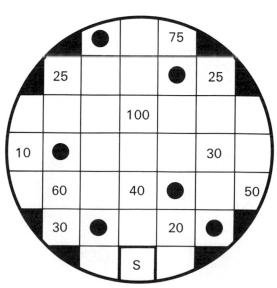

29 Happy numbers!

The number 4599 is said to be 'happy', for on finding the sum of the squares of its digits, and then the sum of the squares of the digits of that sum, and so on, the process ends in 1.

$$4599 \rightarrow 4^2 + 5^2 + 9^2 + 9^2 = 203$$
$$203 \rightarrow 2^2 + 0^2 + 3^2 \quad\quad = \;\; 13$$
$$13 \rightarrow 1^2 + 3^2 \quad\quad\quad = \;\; 10$$
$$10 \rightarrow 1^2 + 0^2 \quad\quad\quad = \quad 1$$

Numbers which do not end in 1 after this process are said to be 'sad'.

Investigate! Which numbers are happy? What happens to sad numbers?

30 What is the colour of Anna's hat?

At Zoe's party, Anna, Betty and Candice are standing in line behind each other, with Candice at the back able to see Anna and Betty, Betty in the middle able to see Anna, and Anna at the front unable to see the others. From a collection of two blue and three red paper hats, Zoe places a hat on each of the heads of Anna, Betty and Candice, so they can only see the hats of those in front of them, and do not know which hats are unused. Zoe then asks each of them, in turn, if they know what colour hat they are wearing. Candice, at the back, replies 'No', followed by a 'No' from Betty. But then Anna, who could see none of the hats, was able to give the colour of her hat with confidence. What colour was it?

31 Cubical contortions!

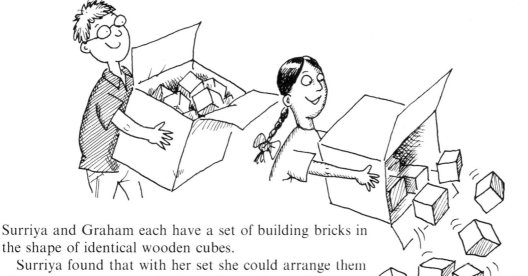

Surriya and Graham each have a set of building bricks in the shape of identical wooden cubes.

Surriya found that with her set she could arrange them all to form a square, or fit them all together to form a larger cube.

Graham, after much experimenting, found that although he could not match Surriya's feat, he could arrange all his bricks to form three squares of different sizes in two distinct ways and, having done that, rearrange them to form two squares.

Assuming that they each possess the smallest number of bricks required to achieve these feats, how many bricks do they each have?

32 Empty the glass!

A helping of ice-cream sits in a Martini glass formed from four matchsticks. Show how to move two matches to reposition the glass so that the ice-cream is no longer in the glass, but outside it.

It ought to be easy!

33 Mum's happy!

Teenage daughter: 'Oh Mum, you are square!'
Mother: 'But I'm happy, and that's what matters!'

How old is mum?

34 A fascinating pentagonal array!

The numbers 1 to 80 can be arranged to form four pentagons, each within the other, so that the three outer pentagons are magic (that is, the sums of the numbers along the side of each pentagon are equal) and, furthermore, the sums of the numbers along each radius through the vertices of all four pentagons are equal.

See if you can complete the array.

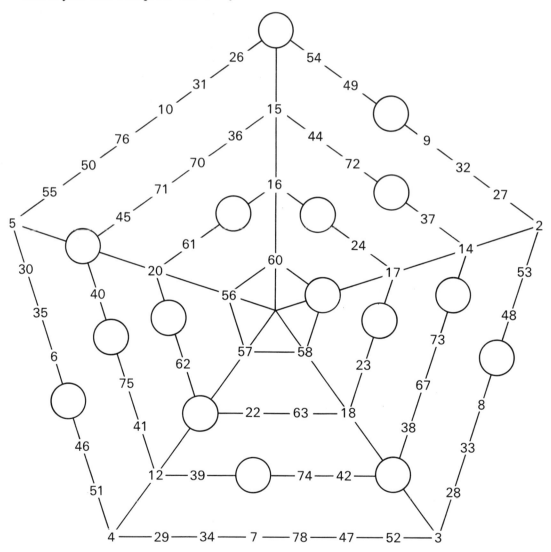

35 Bending Euclid!

Where on earth can you find a triangle each of whose interior angles is 90°?

24

36   Tetrahexagons

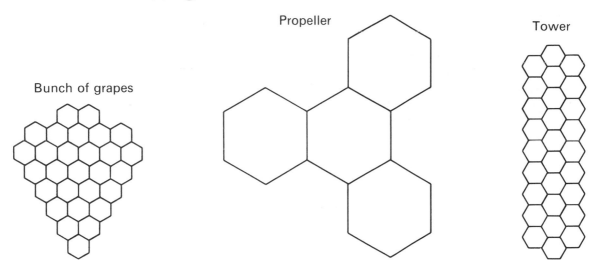

Propeller

Tower

Bunch of grapes

The 'propeller' is one of seven different shapes which can be made by fitting four hexagonal tiles together, edge to edge, as shown. Find the other six such shapes and cut the seven shapes out of thin card. The challenge now is to fit them together, like a jigsaw, to make the bunch of grapes and the tower shown.

37   Bowler of the match?

When New South Wales played cricket against Victoria at Sydney in 1906–07, C. G. Macartney and M. A. Noble had the following bowling analyses:

   1st innings: Macartney 2 for 43   Noble 1 for 32
   2nd innings: Macartney 4 for 6   Noble 6 for 21

Who had the better bowling average in the first innings?
Who had the better bowling average in the second innings?
Who should be awarded the title 'Bowler of the Match'?

38 Knight's tours!

There are many traditional problems concerning the finding of routes on squared boards which a chess knight could take to visit each square only once. The boards given here are shapes with a difference but the problem is the same. Start where you like and try to find a route which visits each square once. With two of the shapes it is possible to find a route which finishes the knight's move from the starting square. Such a route is known as a *re-entrant tour*.

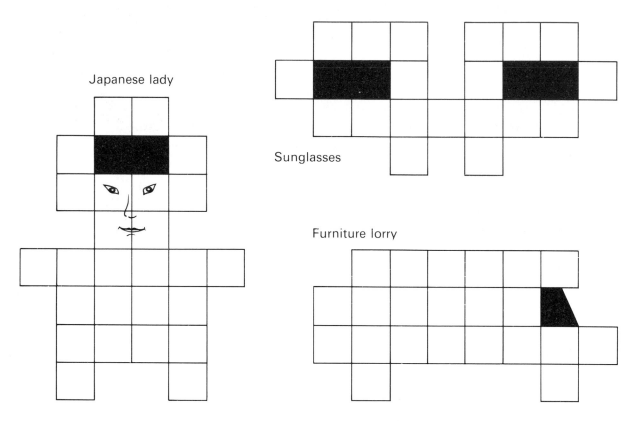

Japanese lady

Sunglasses

Furniture lorry

39 Ornithology!

Replace each different letter by a different digit to make the sum add up.

```
    T I T
  W R E N
+ R O B I N
  B I R D S
```

26

40 Skimming across the river!

Peter often passed away time skimming pebbles across the nearby river above the weir, where the water was still and deep. From his observations, Peter reckoned that each bounce of the pebble was half the length of the previous one. He found he could easily skim a pebble the full width of the river whenever the first bounce landed more than halfway across the river. However, he was determined to succeed when the first bounce landed exactly halfway across, and persisted in trying. If Peter succeeds in skimming a pebble so that its first bounce does land exactly halfway across, how many bounces will it take for the pebble to reach the other side of the river?

41 Digital dance!

Which six-figure number, all of whose digits are different, has the property that when it is multiplied by any of the integers 1, 2, 3, 4, 5 or 6, the resultant product is another six-figure number containing the same set of digits?

42 Two's enough!

Can you find a way of colouring in twelve of the small squares of the 6 × 6 board so that there are two coloured squares in each row and each column, and no more than two on any diagonal line.

43 A pentomino game

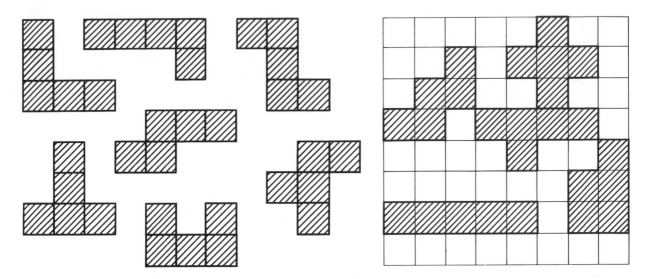

Readers of this book are probably familiar with the twelve pentominoes, the shapes formed by fitting five squares together edge to edge. For convenience, they are all shown in the figure. You will need a set of them to play this game, which is played on an 8 × 8 board, like a chessboard, where the squares are of a size compatible with those of the pentominoes. Two players take it in turns to add a pentomino to the board. The first player unable to fit a pentomino into the remaining spaces loses. Have a go; it is a thought-provoking game!

44 Patterns to appreciate

$$0 \times 9 + 1 = 1$$
$$1 \times 9 + 2 = 11$$
$$12 \times 9 + 3 = 111$$
$$123 \times 9 + 4 = 1\,111$$
$$1\,234 \times 9 + 5 = 11\,111$$
$$12\,345 \times 9 + 6 = 111\,111$$
$$123\,456 \times 9 + 7 = 1\,111\,111$$
$$1\,234\,567 \times 9 + 8 = 11\,111\,111$$
$$12\,345\,678 \times 9 + 9 = 111\,111\,111$$
$$123\,456\,789 \times 9 + 10 = 1\,111\,111\,111$$

Investigate a similar number pattern where the first two lines are:

$$1 \times 8 + 1 = 9$$
$$12 \times 8 + 2 = 98$$

45 Make yourself a ruled surface

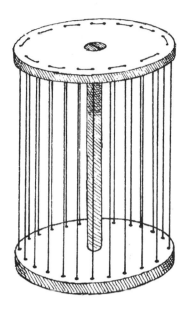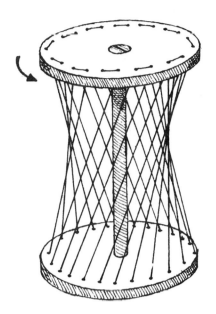

Take two discs of plywood, hardboard or thick card about 8 cm in diameter and drill 24 small holes equally spread around the circumference. Metal lids from old paint tins could also be used, although you could buy the plywood bases used in cane work from a craft shop. Now screw the discs through their centres to the ends of a piece of dowel about 15 cm long. Thread shirring elastic through the discs so that the elastic is parallel to the dowel as shown in the left-hand diagram. The effect is that of a circular cylinder.

Now hold the bottom disc and turn the top disc. The effect will be to pull the shirring elastic at an angle and the lines they form will appear to all lie on a curved surface known as a 'hyperboloid'.

This surface is called a ruled surface because of the way the straight lines lie in it. Contrast this with the surface of a sphere, for example, on which straight lines are impossible.

You will probably recognise the surface as that of the giant cooling towers seen at some electricity power stations. It is also the shape which a soap film takes up when it forms between two wire rings.

46 Knotted!

Take a thin strip of paper, say 30 cm by 2 cm. Hold it at the ends and give one end three half-turns before joining the two ends together with sticky tape. You should now have a band rather like a figure of eight shown. This band has many interesting properties. One is that if you cut the band down its middle along its length, the result is 'a single band of double the length of the original with a knot in it'! Try it and see!

47 The windmill

Use all 28 dominoes from a standard double-six set to make the design shown, making sure that where two dominoes join, their numbers match.

48 Prime addresses!

Professor Newton and her friend Dr Lagrange lived in the same avenue with only four houses between them. The numbers of their houses were both prime, which appealed to them as mathematicians, and when Professor Newton found that she could express the number of her house as the sum of the squares of the two digits of her friend's number she was over the moon! She also noted that their ages were ten years less than their house numbers.

So what were the numbers of their houses, and how old were Professor Newton and Dr Lagrange?

49 Exercising Bouncer!

Matt and his dog Bouncer were walking along the beach to meet their friend Lina. They first spotted her when she was 4 km away and waved their recognition. Bouncer immediately set off to greet Lina, bounding along at 30 km per hour. But on reaching her he turned around and raced back to Matt, then back to Lina, then back to Matt, and so on until they were all together. If Matt walked at 4.5 km per hour and Lina at 3.5 km per hour, how far did Bouncer run in his journeys between them?

50 An ancient riddle

When first the marriage knot was tied between my wife and me,
Her age did mine as far exceed, as three plus three exceeds three;
But when three years and half three years we man and wife had been
Our ages were in ratio then as twelve is to thirteen.

How old were they on their wedding day?

51 Double glazed!

Looking at the architect's drawing for the house they hoped to have built, Mr and Mrs Pretentious decided that the proposed window in the downstairs cloakroom was too large. The architect had designed it to be a metre square. They still wanted it to be square, but half the area. When the architect returned, having carried out their wishes, the window was still a metre wide and a metre high! How could that be?

52 Esther's dilemma

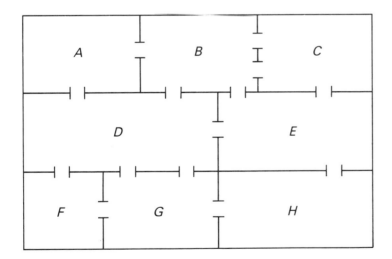

Esther McDougall lived on the ground floor of a very old Scottish manor house. It had no corridors, but access between rooms was easily made using the many connecting doorways. Since an early age Esther had often set herself the task, on a cold winter's day, of trying to find a route around her abode which passed through each of the internal doorways once only. She is getting very frustrated at her lack of success and would dearly like to know whether or not a route is possible. Can you help her?

53 Tic-tac-toe

This game comes in many forms but its roots can be traced
back to Egypt in 1300 BC, and records of it can be found in
China as far back as 500 BC. In this version the board
consists of a square, its diagonals, and the lines bisecting its
opposite sides. The key places are the nine points of
intersection. Each player has three counters (or coins),
which are identifiable, and these are played in turn onto
any vacant point until all six pieces are in play. The aim is
for a player to obtain a straight line of three with their
counters. When all the counters are on the board, play
continues by players moving their pieces, one at a time, to
any vacant adjacent point along a line.

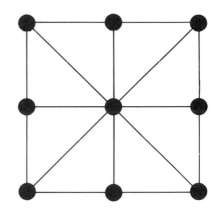

54 Piling up the ancestors!

Suppose that, going back in time, you have a new
generation of ancestors on average every 25 years. Then

25 years ago you had 2 ancestors, your parents
50 years ago you had 4 ancestors, your grandparents
75 years ago you had 8 ancestors, your
                         great-grandparents

and so on, doubling every 25 years.

This argument suggests that 2000 years ago you would
have had

2^{80} ancestors.

That is approximately

1 200 000 000 000 000 000 000 000 ancestors,

a number far larger than everyone who has ever lived.
Where is the flaw in this argument?

55 Equal shares for all!

A landowner died leaving his estate, which unusually was in the shape of a square, to be shared among his wife and four children. His wife was to have the quarter of the estate indicated by the triangle on the plan, while his will decreed that the four children should share the remaining land in such a way that they each had areas identical in both size and shape.

Help the children determine their inheritance!

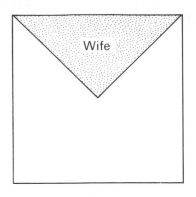

56 Coincident birthdays!

By a rare piece of good fortune, the birthdays of Grandpa Matthew, his son Mark and his grandson Luke all coincided. When Luke was born, Mark realised that his own age and that of his father, an octogenarian, had a prime factor in common. Wondering whether this could happen again, he surmised that it would only be possible if his father lived beyond 100, by which time Luke would be in secondary school and Mark in middle age.

How old would they each be then?

57 Tetraboloes

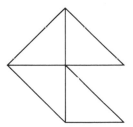 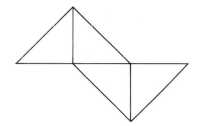 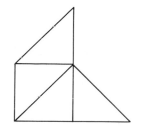

Tetraboloes are the shapes which can be made by joining together four isosceles right-angled triangles (the halves of a square formed by a diagonal, often found as tiles in a set of children's building blocks). The four triangles can be joined along the sides containing the right angle, or along their hypotenuse. Three such shapes are given. How many tetraboloes can you find?

When you think you have them all, make up a set from thin card and use subsets of them to form the three large squares shown.

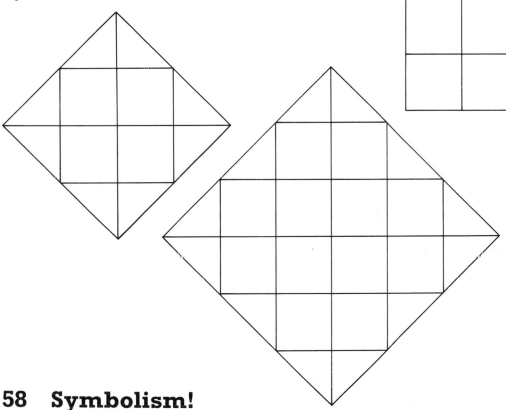

58 Symbolism!

(a) How can you take 1 from 19 to leave 20?

(b) In how many ways can you arrange the symbols 8, 6 and 1 to form a three-digit number divisible by 9?

59 Find the missing money!

Three friends went out for a business lunch and agreed to share the bill. The waiter presented them with a bill for £30 and they each gave him a £10 note. But, having put the money in the till, the waiter realised he had overcharged them. The bill should have been £26, for there was a special offer on the wine which he had overlooked. So he took £4 from the till in order to repay them. However, splitting £4 equally between three people daunted him, so he pocketed £1 and gave £1 to each of the friends. Thus each friend had paid £9, and between them £27. But the waiter only had £1 in his pocket, making a total of £28. So what happened to the £2?

60 Manipulating calendar digits

The 'Four 4s' problem challenges you to express all the integers from 1 to 100 using all four 4 digits, and any mathematical symbol known to you, in each case. An interesting and challenging variation on this theme is to take the four digits of the current year and use them instead of four 4s. The first time I tried this was in 1985, and I was eventually able to complete my century, but only after returning to the problem several times. Here are some of my solutions:

$$6 = 91 - 85 \qquad\qquad 10 = (18 \times 5)/9$$
$$17 = 1 + 5 + 8 + \sqrt{9} \qquad 30 = (9 + 1)(8 - 5)$$
$$64 = 8(5 + \sqrt{9}) \times 1 \qquad 70 = (9 \times 8) - (1/0.5)$$

More recently I have been trying to do the same with 1992, and have managed to express 1 to 50 always using a 1, two 9s and a 2, and restricting the mathematical symbols to $+$, $-$, $\times$, $\div$, $\sqrt{}$, brackets and decimal points. I challenge you to do the same!

61　The square pack

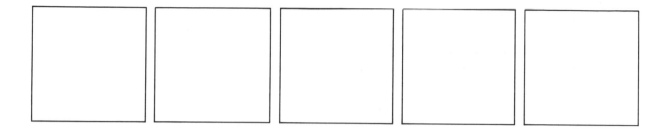

Given five identical square pieces of card, how can you
make one straight cut which will enable you to rearrange
all the resulting pieces into one large square?

62　The hangover!

Three student friends Karen, Pete and Lynn held a party in
their flat to celebrate the end of their exams. They had each
contributed eight bottles of wine for the party, and when
they came to clear up the next day they found seven
unopened bottles, seven half-full bottles and ten empty
bottles. How can they each acquire eight bottles which give
them a fair share of the wine remaining, without resorting
to pouring any of the wine from one bottle to another?

63　Extrapolating from five
seconds!

(a) A clock strikes six in five seconds.
　　How long does it take to strike twelve?

(b) If five ladybirds devour five greenfly in five seconds,
　　how many ladybirds are required to devour a hundred
　　greenfly in a hundred seconds?

64 Three square units

The polygon shown, made from twelve matchsticks, has an area of 5 square units, where the unit of length is taken as the length of a matchstick. It is easy to form other polygons, using all twelve matchsticks, with the same area but can you find such polygons with an area of 3 square units? Many ingenious solutions are possible, so see what you can find.

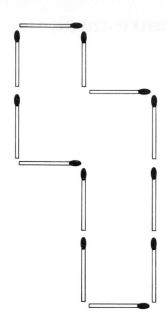

65 Magic tetrahedra

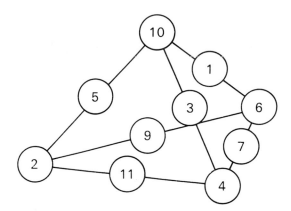

In the tetrahedron shown the three numbers along each edge sum to 17, making it magic.

Using any ten numbers from the set of integers from 1 to 11, see how many distinctly different magic tetrahedra you can find.

What is the lowest magic total you can find using these numbers?

Can you find a magic tetrahedron using only the integers from 1 to 10?

66 Fault-free rectangles

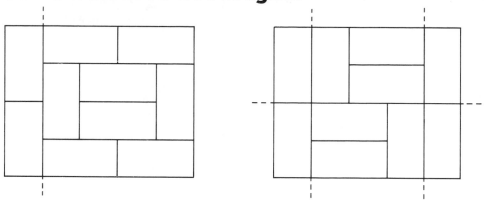

Imagine you have a large supply of 2 × 1 blocks (dominoes are ideal) and that you are investigating ways of fitting them together to make rectangles. For example, two ways of making a 5 × 4 rectangle are shown. But in each case there is what is known as a fault line in the pattern indicated by the dotted lines. These are straight lines corresponding to the edges of the blocks which cut right across the rectangle, and are seen as a weakness. Unfortunately the 5 × 4 rectangle cannot be made without at least one fault line.

The challenge here is to find which rectangles can be formed without a fault line, and particularly to find the dimensions of the smallest such rectangle and square.

67 Dr Shah in the country

While Dr Shah was walking with her nephew Ravi in the country, their way was barred by a wide river. Dr Shah challenged Ravi to measure the width of the river without getting wet. Ravi protested that he had no instruments but Dr Shah assured him that, with a little thought and some exercise, he would be able to measure the width of the river, in terms of his paces, quite easily. Ravi succeeded. Would you have done? Of course there was no bridge!

68 In their prime

Mr and Mrs Babbage first met when they were pupils at secondary school. In 1994 they celebrated the wedding of their youngest daughter, Rachel. Being fascinated by numbers, Mr Babbage was delighted to note that, at that time, both his and his wife's ages, and Rachel's too, could be expressed in the form p^3q, where p and q are prime numbers. He reckoned that such a propitious occurrence augured well for the occasion. Given that Mr Babbage is younger than his wife, can you find the years in which each of the three were born?

69 Which way to Birminster's spire?

The church spires of Ablethorpe, Birminster, Canchester and Dukesbury are each visible from the others on a clear day. The spire of Ablethorpe church is the same distance from Birminster's as Canchester's is from Birminster's, and Dukesbury's from Canchester's. Furthermore, the church spires of Canchester and Dukesbury are the same distance from Ablethorpe's as Birminster's is from Dukesbury's.

Given that Dukesbury is due east of Ablethorpe, and that Canchester is further north than either of these towns, can you find the bearing of Birminster's spire from that of Ablethorpe?

70 Unit fractions

Find natural numbers x, y, z such that

$$\frac{1}{x} + \frac{1}{y} + \frac{1}{z} = \frac{1}{5}$$

where $x < y < z$

You may be surprised at just how many solutions exist.

71 Paper tearing!

Take a sheet of any newspaper. Tear it in half and put the two pieces together. Now tear the two pieces in half and put them on top of each other to form a pile of four pieces. Tear the four pieces in half and put them on top of each other to form a pile of eight pieces. Imagine yourself repeating this process 40 times, always doubling the number of pieces of paper in your pile.

How high do you think your pile would be at the end of the process?

72 A devilish domino distribution!

Draw yourself an 8 × 8 squared board to match the size of your dominoes, so that a domino covers exactly two squares. The 28 dominoes from a standard set can be placed on the board to cover all but eight of the squares in many ways. One way is shown which leaves just one square uncovered in each row and column of the board. There are several ways of doing this which you may try, but the real challenge is to find a way where, in addition, no three of the centres of the uncovered squares lie in a straight line.

The distribution of the dominoes in the solution shown fails on two counts, indicated by the lines through the centres of the offending squares.

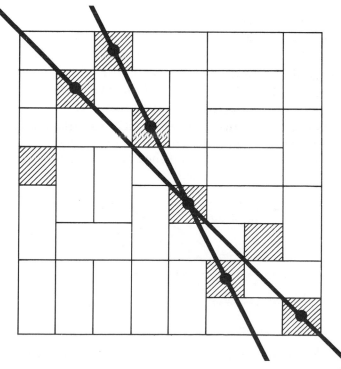

73 Tri-hex

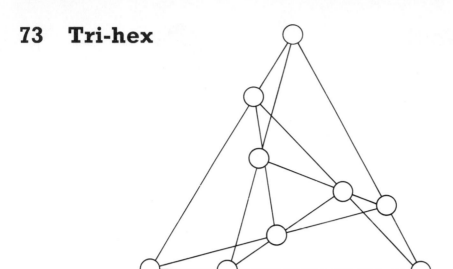

This is a version of noughts and crosses for two players. To play it, make a playing area marked out as shown and obtain two sets of coloured counters, four of each colour. (Coins make a good alternative to counters.) Each player takes it in turn to place a counter of their colour on an unoccupied circle. The winner of the game is the first player to get three counters in a straight line.

74 Mr Mailshot's muddle

In making up a mail order for three customers, Mr Mailshot realised he had put the wrong address labels on each of the parcels. Mrs Ambridge had ordered two red crystal balls and Mr Beaufort had ordered two blue crystal balls, while Miss Clapham had ordered one red and one blue crystal ball. Each of the balls had been packed separately in identical boxes before being wrapped up into the customers' parcels. How many parcels and how many individual balls will Mr Mailshot have to inspect before he can correctly relabel them?

75 Staggering!

From his years of experience, Joe Greensward, the groundsman at Ivy League College, knew the precise length of the stagger between the lanes for a 400 m race on a 400 m track. So when he had to mark in the staggers on the prestigious new 200 m all-weather track for a 400 m race he argued as follows:

The track is half as long, which will imply half the stagger I usually use, but now they have to do two laps for a 400 m race, so I will need to double it, which means it will be just the same as I have used on the 400 m track.

As he watched the 400 m race in the inaugural athletic meeting, he hung his head in shame when he realised that the 400 m runners only kept to their lanes in the first lap.
  What should he do?

76 The queen's pursuit

In the course of a game of chess, the black king and the white queen were in the positions shown on the board. In the ensuing game the queen relentlessly pursued the king, who was pinned to the spot. In doing so, she visited all the other squares on the board, having made the smallest number of changes of direction as possible, before ending up beside him. What route does the queen take?

43

77 Ageing!

This is a way of determining someone's age by a devious means, but will only work if they are willing to take part by carrying out the given set of computations, using a calculator if required.

1 Add 1 to the number of the month in which you were born.
2 Multiply by 100.
3 Add the day of the month in which you were born.
4 Multiply by 2.
5 Add 11.
6 Multiply by 5.
7 Add 50.
8 Multiply by 10.
9 Add your age.
10 Add 61.

Now ask for the resulting number and subtract 11 111; the pairs of digits from the right give the person's age, day of the month in which they were born, and birth month.

Check it out on yourself before trying it out on someone else. How does it work?

78 Follow my leader?

Two people are 10 miles apart when they set off in the same direction and travel at the same speed for two hours, by which time they are 22 miles apart.

How can this be? What is their likely mode of travel?

79 The disappearing act!

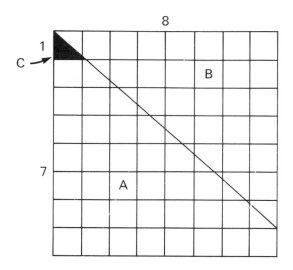
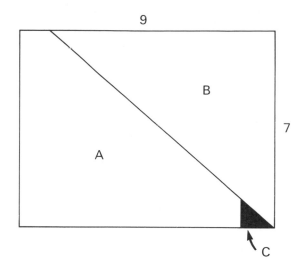

Take a piece of squared paper and carefully cut out an
8 × 8 square. Next cut the square into three pieces as
shown. Take the small triangle C to the bottom right-hand
corner of A, and then slide B along the diagonal to form a
9 × 7 rectangle.

The original square had an area of 8 × 8 = 64 square
units, but the rectangle only has an area of 9 × 7 = 63
square units. What happened to the missing square unit?

80 The missing digit!

Here is a trick you can play with your friends. Ask them to
think of a four-digit number, and then to subtract from it
each of the number's digits. So if, for example, your friend
chooses 2508 and then takes away 2, 5, 0 and 8, the
resultant number will be 2493. Next invite your friend to
give you all but one of the digits of the new number and
you will be able to supply the missing digit. How can you
possibly do this?

81 Romantic?

From six you take nine
And from nine you take ten
Then from forty take fifty
And six will remain.

82 Mustafa's pride and joy!

Chief Mustafa's pride and joy were his eleven fine white oxen. After his death, his principal wife made it known that her late husband wanted the oxen shared between his three eldest sons, Yusuf, Raheem and Ibrahim, so that they have $\frac{1}{2}$, $\frac{1}{4}$ and $\frac{1}{6}$ respectively. Not wanting to end up with having to dissect any of the beautiful beasts, they consulted the village oracle. She soon put them out of their misery by adding her one and only ox to the eleven and then giving six to Yusuf, three to Raheem, two to Ibrahim, and finally taking her own back! There is surely something strange going on here. Can you make sense of it?

83 Common factors

Arrange the following nine numbers into a 3 × 3 array so that the numbers in any row, column or diagonal have just one prime number factor in common:

65   77   95   187   266   273   330   442   969

84 Fill the gap!

Find the missing number.

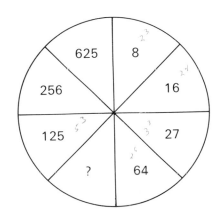

46

85 Who do you know?

It is an interesting fact that

if a room contains six people, then either there will be at least three people who all know each other or there will be at least three people who have no knowledge of each other.

The reasoning is as follows:

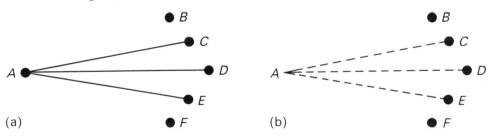

(a)   (b)

Let six people be represented by points *A, B, C, D, E, F,* as shown. Let a line joining two points represent that they know each other, and a broken line that they do not know each other.

Consider *A*'s relation to the others. There are two cases to consider: (a) *A* knows at least three other people; (b) *A* knows fewer than three other people.

Case (a) Suppose *A* knows *C, D* and *E*. Then
either *C* knows *D*, or *D* knows *E*, or *E* knows *C*, in which case *A* will form one vertex of a triangle bounded by 'know lines',
or none of *C, D* or *E* will know each other.

Case (b) If *A* knows fewer than three other people, then *A* will not know at least three people. Suppose *C, D* and *E* are not known by *A*, then
either *C* doesn't know *D*, or *D* doesn't know *E*, or *E* doesn't know *C*, in which case *A* will form one vertex of a triangle bounded by 'don't know' lines,
or all of *C, D* and *E* will know each other.

47

86 Cross-out

1	2	3	4	5	6	7	8	9

This is a game for two or more players played with a pair of standard dice.

On a piece of paper draw a line of boxes and enter the numbers 1 to 9 as shown.

The first player throws the dice and computes their total. If, for example, the total is 8, then the player can cross out the 8 or any two numbers totalling 8: say 7 and 1, or 6 and 2, or 5 and 3. The first player continues throwing the two dice and crossing out a single number or pair of numbers until the three highest numbers are crossed out, after which only one dice is thrown at a time. When a player is unable to match the total on the dice to an uncrossed number or pair of numbers, then the total of the uncrossed numbers is found and becomes that person's score. Each player takes it in turn to play in the same way and the winner will be the one with the lowest score.

87 Joe Joiner's new bench

Joe Joiner decided he needed a new working surface and, looking around his workshop, he found four pieces of timber each 20 cm wide and 3 cm thick, with lengths of 150 cm, 180 cm, 210 cm and 270 cm respectively. After some thought, he was able to use these pieces to make himself a rectangular bench top with enough timber to make three strengthening battens stretching the full width of the top. He achieved this with only three saw-cuts, and without wasting any timber.

What are the dimensions of Joe's new working surface?

88 Partitioning the plantation

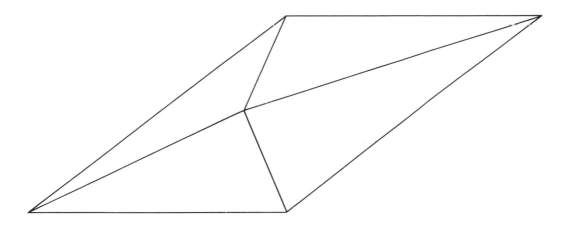

Lord Evergreen celebrated his 80th birthday by giving his four children one of his valuable plantations, which was in the shape of a parallelogram. He stipulated that his eldest son and daughter should each have a 30% share, and his younger son and daughter a 20% share. They were each to have triangular plots with one common corner, and he gave his estate manager the task of marking the boundaries and allocating the plots. Where will the common corner be, and how many different ways could the estate manager allocate the plots?

89 When was Professor Danzig born?

Professor Danzig enjoyed looking for patterns in numbers, and on her birthday in 1992 she was particularly pleased when she realised that her age in years multiplied by the day in the year came to 11 111.

When was she born?

90 This number is unique!

There is just one number whose square and cube, between them, use up each of the ten digits 0, 1, 2, 3, . . . 9 only once.

Can you find it?

91 Triangular animals!

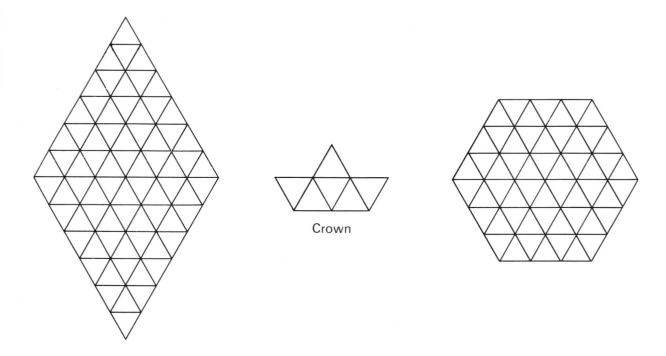

Crown

Shapes formed by fitting triangular tiles together are often referred to as 'triangular animals'. You are challenged to find all the different triangular animals you can using six triangles. One of the animals, known as the 'crown', is given to start you off.

Make cut-outs from thin card of the animals you have found and then try to fit them together, jigsaw fashion, to cover the diamond and hexagon shown. You will need all the possible shapes to cover the diamond, but the hexagon only needs nine of your animals.

92 Multiplication magic

$$41\,096 \times 83 = 3\,410\,968$$

To multiply 41 096 by 83, all you need to do is to enclose 41 096 with the 3 and 8 as shown. The same trick works if 41 096 is prefixed by the sequence of digits 41095890 repeated any number of times. For example,

$$4\,109\,589\,041\,096 \times 83 = \mathbf{341\,095\,890\,410\,968}$$
$$410\,958\,904\,109\,589\,041\,096 \times 83 = \mathbf{34\,109\,589\,041\,095\,890\,410\,968}$$

Fascinating, but hardly worth committing to memory!

93 Adventure holidays!

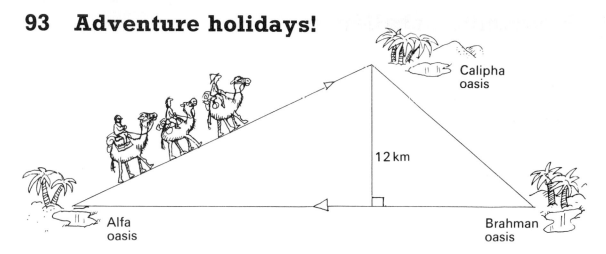

As the highlight of an adventure holiday, the intrepid travellers left the Alfa oasis with their camels heading, or so they thought, straight out across the inhospitable desert towards the Brahman oasis. But their overconfident leader had followed the wrong caravan trail and they found themselves at the Calipha oasis, which was 12 km from the straight line route they should have taken. The local people at Calipha soon put them right, and they were soon able to head straight for the Brahman oasis, thankful that it was a shorter journey than they had so far come. Refreshed, they then took the direct route back to Alfa, none the worse for wear and with a good story to bore their friends with when they got home. Given that the round trip was 54 km, and that the distances between each of the three oases is a whole number of kilometres, find out how far apart they are.

94 Cross out nine digits

Given the addition sum

$$
\begin{array}{r}
111 \\
333 \\
+\ 555 \\
777 \\
999 \\
\hline
\end{array}
$$

you are challenged to cross out nine of the digits so that the total of the numbers remaining is 1111.

The solution is not unique. See how many ways you can do it.

95 A sequential challenge

5 1 18 12 14 4 13 7 19 16 20 6

The sequence of twelve integers shown contains within it some increasing sequences of five numbers (for example 5, 12, 13, 19, 20) and a decreasing sequence of five numbers (18, 14, 13, 7, 6).

Rearrange the numbers so that the sequence you form does not contain any increasing or decreasing sequences of five numbers.

Now, using any integers you like, find the longest possible sequence which does not contain any increasing or decreasing sequences of five numbers.

96 Fencing!

Joe Appleyard wanted to build a fence to protect his orchard. The fence was to be built 90 m down one side of a valley and 78 m up the other side. The slope of the valley sides are shown, together with the heights of the valley sides above the valley's bottom. The fencing panels are 2 m long and 1.5 m high. How many panels will be needed?

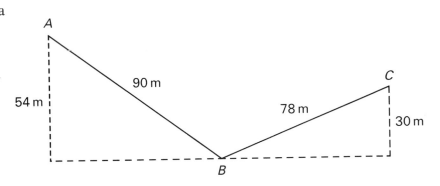

97 Triangular Nim

Place 15 coins (or counters) to form a triangular array as shown. Two players take it in turn to remove a single coin or all of the coins in a row. The person forced to pick up the last coin is the loser. Have fun!

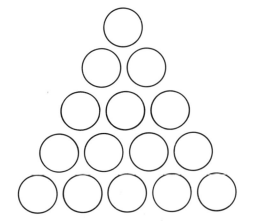

98 Bridge that gap!

In the grounds of an outward bound school there was a circular pond of radius 20 m with an island in the centre on which stood a fountain. One of the initiative tests for the participants in the school's courses was to construct a bridge from the edge of the pond to the island using only two planks, each of length 4.9 m. They found the test very frustrating, for the closest point of the island to the edge of the pond was 5 m, and they frequently lost their planks in the water. But a practical solution is possible. Can you find it?

99 Customs control!

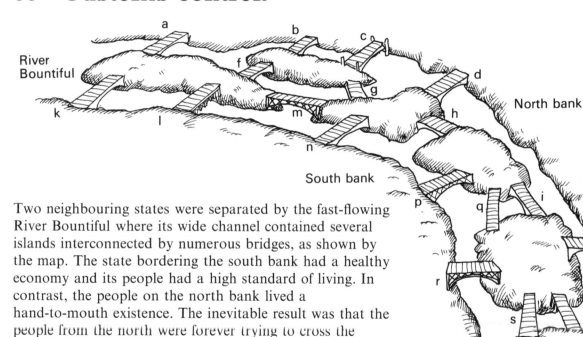

Two neighbouring states were separated by the fast-flowing River Bountiful where its wide channel contained several islands interconnected by numerous bridges, as shown by the map. The state bordering the south bank had a healthy economy and its people had a high standard of living. In contrast, the people on the north bank lived a hand-to-mouth existence. The inevitable result was that the people from the north were forever trying to cross the bridges to the south.

Because of this the neighbouring states had agreed to staff all the bridges with customs officers. Their initial plan envisaged the minimum number of officers required at each bridge as: a = 8, b = 7, c = 4, d = 8, e = 10, f = 3, g = 9, h = 4, i = 6, j = 7, k = 9, l = 8, m = 5, n = 6, p = 2, q = 3, r = 5, s = 4, t = 8. But there was no way they could find so many qualified officers. Luckily one of the planners realised that they were being foolish, for it was possible to control the flow between the north and south bank by staffing fewer than half the bridges.

What is the smallest number of officers which could be used, and at which bridges would they be deployed?

100 Magic!

A conjuror arranged before his audience a line of seven identical boxes, in each of which were a number of coloured balls. He invited his audience to give him any number N from 1 to 24, and he would then be able to tip out either a single box containing N balls or an adjacent set of boxes which between them contained N balls.

How many balls did each box contain?

It may help you to know that no number N from 1 to 24 required more than five boxes to be emptied!

101 Save the farmer's legs!

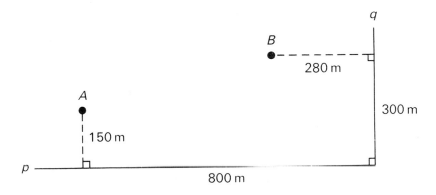

Farmer Broadacres was out in his large pasture at A (see the diagram) when he decided to check up on the two electric fences p and q, which formed part of the field boundary, before inspecting the well at B. What is the shortest route he could take to visit each fence and end up at the well?

102 Quadrupled!

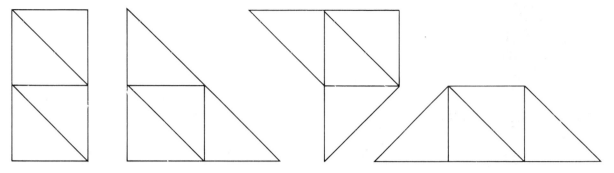

The four shapes shown, each of which can be thought of as
consisting of four half-squares, can be put together like the
pieces of a jigsaw in four different ways to reproduce larger
versions of themselves. Cut out the shapes from card and
see if you can reproduce their enlargements.

103 A painless deduction!

Can you find a way of taking 45 away from 45 so that 45
remains?

104 Matchstick magic

Starting with the arrangement
of 13 matchsticks shown, can
you:

(*a*) remove two matches to
leave just four triangles;

(*b*) remove three matches to
leave just four triangles;

(*c*) remove four matches to
leave just five triangles;

(*d*) remove three matches to
leave just three triangles?

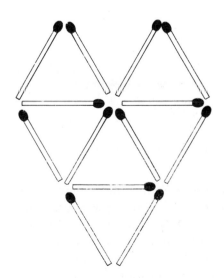

105 Two special square numbers

What are the smallest and largest square numbers to contain each of the ten digits 0, 1, 2, . . . 9?

106 Locomotion!

Dr Fit and his niece Razia were travelling on an intercity train at over 100 mph. To amuse his niece, Dr Fit gave her a problem to think about. Could Razia jump further along the carriage aisle if she jumped in the direction the train was moving, or if she jumped in the opposite direction?

107 How numerate are you?

$$9 + \frac{99}{99} = 10$$

Find ten further ways of expressing 10 as a combination of five 9s, where they can be combined using familiar arithmetic operations.

108 Reservoir revelations!

The local water company wanted to build a new storage tank to supply the needs of a large housing estate. They calculated that they needed the tank to have a capacity of $8000 \, m^3$, and they decided to construct it as an open-top rectangular tank. It was to be made from reinforced concrete panels whose cost was proportional to the interior surface area of the tank.

What shape should they make it to minimise the cost?

109 Domestic deliberations!

Percy Porker and his wife Pansy had some important
decisions to make about their herd of pigs. Percy, the
interminable pessimist, was concerned about their supply of
food so he proposed to sell 75 of their pigs, which would
mean their food would last 20 days longer than if they did
nothing. Pansy, on the other hand, was eager to increase
the size of their herd by buying an extra 100 pigs. She
argued that this would only decrease by 15 days the time
which they could feed all their pigs for, and she was
optimistic that they would be able to obtain more food.

How many pigs do the Porkers have?

110 Target

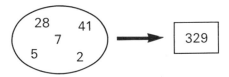

This is a game based on one used in some television quiz
shows. The participants are given a three-digit target
number and a set of two- and single-digit numbers. They
are then challenged to combine all or some of the numbers
from the set with $+$, $-$, $\times$, $\div$ and brackets as needed, to
get as close to the target as possible. The nearest to the
target is awarded a point, with a bonus point for a
bull's-eye. For example, with the target 329 and the
numbers given, competitors might obtain

$$(5 + 7) \times 28 - 2 = 334$$
$$(28 \div 7) \times 2 \times 41 = 328$$
$$(41 + 28) \times 5 - (7 \times 2) = 331$$

and the second competitor would be awarded a point.

Can you do better?

111 Back-packing!

This is a riddle attributed to Euclid from AD 300.

A mule and a donkey were walking along laden with sacks of corn. The mule said to the donkey, 'If you gave me one of your sacks, I would be carrying twice as much as you. But if I gave you one, we would both be carrying equal burdens.'

How many sacks of corn were they each carrying?

112 Multiple units!

Investigate the factors of the mono-digit numbers consisting of strings of ones, such as

11   111   1111   11111   111111   . . .

and try to determine which, if any, are prime after 11.

58

113 Dr Sharma's railway riddle

While out with her niece, Emma, Dr Sharma watched an express train snaking along the curved track and pondered over the problem the railway engineers had solved. The problem is best understood by imagining a circular track where the inner radius is R and the distance between the rails is d. The length of the inner rail is $2\pi R$ while that of the outside track is $2\pi(R + d)$. So the wheels on the outside track have to travel $2\pi d$ further than those on the inside track on each circuit. Now Dr Sharma knew that the wheels of railway engines and their rolling stock were firmly attached to their axles, so that the inner wheel and outer wheel on an axle both turned together. How did the engineers overcome the problem of the wheels having to cover different distances, every time the train negotiated a bend, without the wheels slipping?

   She knew the solution and explained it carefully to Emma, but would you have known?

114 Batting exploits

County cricket in Middleshire was taken very seriously and each individual's results studied in great detail after every match. In one match early in the season, Slogger and Missun, two of the county's favourite players, each scored 33 before being caught out. This has the effect of lowering Slogger's batting average by one run, but raising Missun's average by one. If, before this match, Slogger had scored twice as many runs as Missun and they had each had the same number of innings, what are their new batting averages?

115 How far to the lighthouse?

From the look-out point on the oil tanker, 18 m above the water-line, the light of the Shark Ridge lighthouse flashed into view, just visible above the far horizon. At this state of the tide the light was 34 m above the water. Taking the radius of the Earth as 6400 km, how far was the tanker from the lighthouse?

116 How long is the ladder?

Two ladders of equal length are hinged at one end and stand as an inverted V, with their bottom ends 4 m apart. When a person climbs 3 m up one of the ladders, the rung he stands on is as far from the top of the ladder as it is from the bottom of the opposite ladder.

How long are the ladders?

117 Convex pentagons are out!

What is the largest number of points it is possible to put in a plane so that no three points are collinear, and no five form the vertices of a convex pentagon?

118 A healthy diet!

Confirm this slogan by replacing each different letter by a different digit to form a correct sum.

$$
\begin{array}{r}
BAKED \\
+\ BEANS \\
\hline
FIBRE
\end{array}
$$

119 A game to make you think!

Two players A and B take it in turn to write down a number, less than a hundred, on a piece of paper. A player loses when, having recorded a number, the other player identifies two subsets of the numbers so far recorded which have the same total.

Suppose, for example, the players have recorded

19   2   27   39   5   11

after six turns, with A playing first, and B having just recorded 11. If A is wide awake, he will spot that

$$19 + 27 = 2 + 39 + 5$$

and be the winner.

Interestingly, this game should never go beyond ten moves for it can be shown that, given any ten numbers less than 100, there will always be two subsets of them which have the same total. Why?

Nuptial flight!

Bhaskara, writing in AD 1150, produced an interesting collection of puzzles including the following:

The square root of half the number of bees in a swarm has flown into a jasmine bush, while $\frac{8}{9}$ of the whole swarm has remained behind. One amorous female bee flies about a male bee that is buzzing within a lotus flower into which he was allured in the night by its sweet odour, but he is now imprisoned in it. Tell me the number of bees in the swarm.

121 Hexomino doubles!

All the given hexomino shapes can be made by using the
same subset of four of them. The shapes will have four
times the area of the original, of course, but which four will
you need to choose and how do you fit them together?

122 Coin cutting!

Arrange ten coins or counters
to form a triangular array as
shown. What is the smallest
number of coins you can
remove from this array so
that no three coins have their
centres at the vertices of an
equilateral triangle?

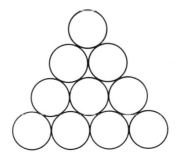

123 The photo cubes!

Miss Telfoto was a keen photographer as well as a creator of three-dimensional puzzles. She set about creating a puzzle in the following way.

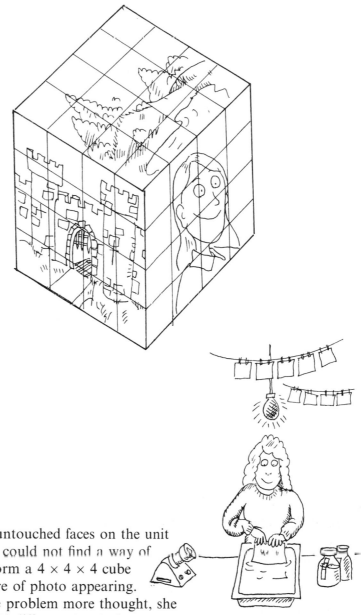

Starting with 64 unit cubes she built a 4 × 4 × 4 larger cube. Then she took six photos, which she had enlarged to be the same size as a face of the large cube, and carefully stuck them onto the faces of the large cube. Next she used a sharp knife to cut the photos along all the lines of the unit cubes so that each photo was divided into small squares corresponding to the faces of the unit cubes. Realising she had many untouched faces of the unit cubes she rearranged them so that she again had a 4 × 4 × 4 cube without a photo square in sight. Taking another six photos she repeated her earlier procedure of sticking one to each face of the large cube and cutting them into 16 small squares. She knew she still had a lot of untouched faces on the unit cubes but, try as she might, she could not find a way of rearranging the 64 of them to form a 4 × 4 × 4 cube without at least one small square of photo appearing.

However, if she had given the problem more thought, she should have been able to stick 24 different 4 × 4 photos onto the cubes so that every unit cube had all its faces covered by a part of one of the photos, and the 64 cubes would be capable of being put together in four distinct ways to form a large cube with a different photo on each face.

How can it be achieved?

124 Non-intersecting knight's tours

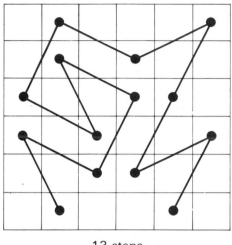

13 steps

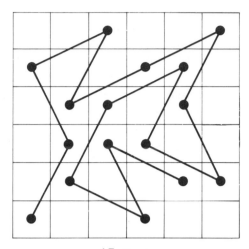

15 steps

Two routes are shown that a chess knight can take on a 6 × 6 board where the path is seen as a sequence of lines joining the centres of the squares connecting each step of the journey. The object is to maximise the number of steps a knight could take on the board consistent with (a) not landing on any square more than once, and (b) ensuring that the path does not cross over itself. The paths shown take 13 and 15 steps respectively. But can you do better?

What is the longest possible path?

Be warned, this is the sort of puzzle on which you can get hooked, and spend many frustrating hours!

125 Calculator challenge

$\frac{239}{169}$ gives $\sqrt{2}$ to an accuracy of 5 significant figures.

What is the smallest pair of integers you can find so that their ratio gives $\sqrt{2}$ to the same accuracy as the square root button on your calculator?

126 Rational cubes

Two cubes are to have a total volume of $17 \, \text{m}^3$. Now there are an infinity of ways of achieving this, but can you find a solution where the edges of both cubes are rational numbers? An exact solution is required, not an approximation!

127   Coin squares

Place 20 coins to form a cross as shown. How many sets of four coins are there in this array which are positioned so that they sit at the corners of a square?

Think carefully before you check the answer at the back, for Professor Hoffman, who first set this puzzle in 1893, gave the answer as 17. But he was wrong!

What is the smallest number of coins you can take away from the array so that no four of the remaining coins are at the vertices of a square?

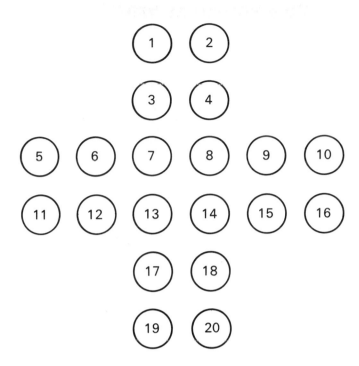

128   Cube rolling!

Make a cube whose square faces are the same size as the squares of your chessboard, or draw up an 8 × 8 board to match the size of an existing cube. Write your name on one face of the cube and place it in one corner of the board with your name on top. The challenge now is to roll the cube, one square at a time (across or up or down but not diagonally), so that it visits every square on the board once and finishes at an adjacent corner to its starting point with your name on top. But your name is not to appear on the top of the cube for any of the intermediate stops!

129 The random walk

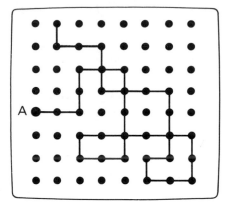

Route length = 35

On the computer screen is an 8 × 8 array of dots. The computer is programmed to trace out a path starting at A. It travels to the right or left or up or down to adjacent dots in a random fashion, although it is not allowed to retrace any part of a path it has already travelled. After it has turned through a right angle 15 times it stops and the length of its path is computed.

What is the longest possible path it could trace out?

130 Net it!

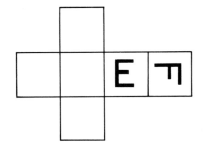

The faces of a die have on them the letters, A, B, C, D, E and F.

Two views of the die are shown, together with a possible net, although only two of the letters have been filled in. Make a drawing of the net, and fill in the letters so that when the net is folded up into the cube it will be identical to that shown.

Easy? Well, now see if you can find a net for the die where all the letters are standing upright!

66

131 A Pythagorean prime property

A prime number which is one more than a multiple of four can uniquely be expressed as the sum of the squares of two numbers which have no factor in common.

For example:

$$5 = \ 1 \times 4 + 1 = 2^2 + 1^2$$
$$29 = \ 7 \times 4 + 1 = 5^2 + 2^2$$
$$53 = 13 \times 4 + 1 = 7^2 + 2^2$$

It follows that any power of such a number will also have the same property, as it will also be one more than a multiple of four.
For example:

$$5^2 = \ 3^2 + \ 4^2$$
$$5^3 = \ 2^2 + 11^2$$
$$5^4 = \ 7^2 + 24^2$$
$$5^5 = 38^2 + 41^2$$

Investigate this surprising property.

132 Flattening a cube efficiently!

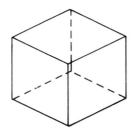
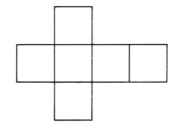
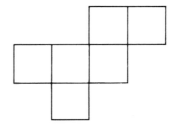

Imagine you have a unit cube made from thin card or paper. It can be cut along its edges in eleven distinct ways and flattened out to form nets consisting of six squares joined by their edges, each a hexomino. In each case the net has a perimeter of 14 units, so the total length of the cut required will be 7 units.

But nets can be made by making some of the cuts across the faces of a cube, such as the one shown here where a pair of opposite faces of a cube have been cut along a diagonal. In this case the length of cut required is $5 + 2\sqrt{2}$ units, which is longer than the 7 units needed for the hexomino nets.

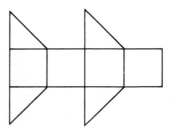

Your challenge is to find ways of cutting the cube, so that it can be flattened, where the total length of cut is as short as possible.

133 Amicable numbers

Two numbers with the property that, for each of them, the sum of all their factors less than themselves is equal to the other number are said to be 'amicable'. One such pair is 1210 and 1184.

The factors of 1210 are 1, 2, 5, 10, 11, 22, 55, 110, 121, 242 and 605, and they sum to 1184, while the factors of 1184 sum to 1210. Only one smaller pair exists and they are both three-digit numbers. Can you find them?

134 Rakesh at the cinema

Rakesh doesn't go to the cinema often, but his father noticed an advert in the local newspaper indicating that one of his favourite old cowboy films was being shown, so he took Rakesh along. They enjoyed the film together, but it gave Rakesh some startling experiences which cried out for an explanation. He was particularly surprised by the stagecoach in one scene. It started off and as it picked up speed its wheels unexpectedly began to rotate backwards, even though it was apparent the stagecoach was moving forwards at ever increasing speed. Then the wheels appeared to become stationary! What is the explanation for this phenomenon?

135 The vertical drop!

An observer watched as a
plane released its food parcels
at great height, one after the
other, as it sped across the
sky. The food parcels
appeared to fall vertically,
directly beneath each other,
yet when they reached the
ground they lay in a long
line. Can you make sense of
this observation?

136 Curves of constant breadth

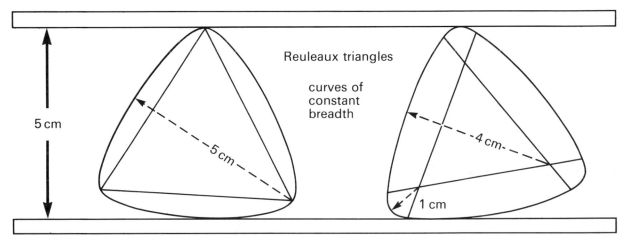

Reuleaux triangles

curves of constant breadth

5 cm

5 cm

4 cm

1 cm

Before meeting these curves for the first time it does not
seem possible that any shape other than a circle would have
the property that, as it rolled along a straight line, its
highest point would be at a constant distance from the line.
Yet an infinity of such curves exist, the 'curves of constant
breadth'. Two of the simplest, known as 'Reuleaux
triangles' after the German engineer, Franz Reuleaux
(1829–1905), who first made a study of them, are shown in
the figure. Cut them out of card, place them between two
rulers placed 5 cm apart, and turn them, noting how they
will always be touching both rulers.

Similar shapes can be made based on regular polygons
with an odd number of sides, and good examples of these
are the British 50p and 20p coins, based on regular
heptagons. Because of their constant breadth property they
can be used in slot machines carefully designed to accept
coins of only one diameter.

50p

20p

But even more astonishing is that if you put your Reuleaux triangles inside a square of side 5 cm, it will remain in contact with all four sides as it is turned! The English engineer H. J. Watts recognised the potential of this property in 1914, using it as the cross-section of a bit for drilling square holes.

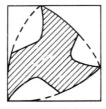

Cross-section of drill in hole

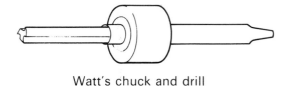

Watt's chuck and drill

What is perhaps very surprising is to find that curves of constant breadth do not even have to have rotational symmetry. One very effective method for constructing such shapes is to start by drawing any number of intersecting lines. Four have been used in the example, labelled l_1, l_2, l_3, l_4. Each arc is then drawn from the point of intersection of the two lines which bound it. For example, this shape was drawn by first drawing arc a_1 with an arbitrary radius centred on A. Arc b_1 was then drawn with centre B, arc c_1 with centre C, arc d_1 with centre D, and so on, adjusting

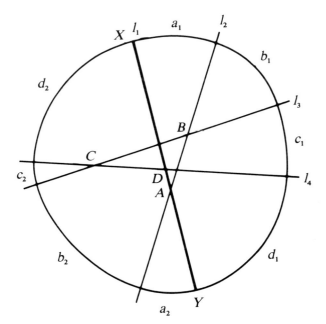

Crossed-line construction of curve of constant breadth

the radius at each stage to ensure the arcs meet. To see why this shape has the required property of constant breadth, consider XY, that part of l_1 cut off by the curve. Rotate it clockwise about A to coincide with l_2, then clockwise about B to coincide with l_3 and finally clockwise about C to coincide with l_4. As l_1 rotates, X and Y trace out the curve and establish the constant width property.

An argument not far removed from the above also establishes the remarkable property that all curves of constant breadth D have a perimeter of πD, the same as a circle with the same diameter!

137 The home stretch!

A spider has made its home in a large empty cubical box in the attic. In each corner of the box it has a nest. What is the minimum length of web the spider could spin so that every nest is interconnected by the web?

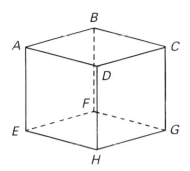

138 Plywood pentominoes!

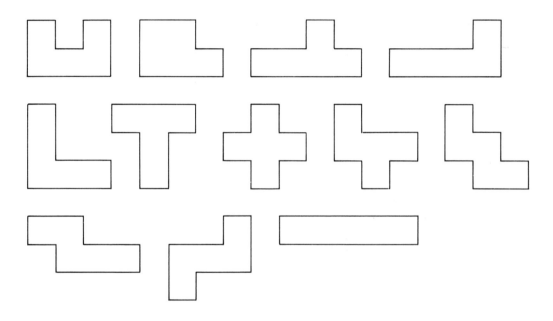

John Makegood was keen to make himself a set of pentominoes by cutting them out of a piece of plywood in the most efficient way. The only saw he had could cut in a straight line, but not around corners, so he wanted to draw up a plan in which the pentominoes were fitted together in a rectangle in such a way that they could be cut out using his saw. He soon satisfied himself that the rectangle would need to have an area of more than 60 square units, and eventually found a way he could produce a set of the twelve pentominoes from a 6 × 13 rectangle. All the cuts could be made with his saw except for the internal cut required for the U-shaped pentomino which he had to do with his one blunt wood chisel. Can you see how John Makegood arranged the pieces, or can you do better?

139 Trisecting an angle

One of the problems posed by the Ancient Greek geometers was to find a ruler and compass construction to trisect any given angle. It taxed the minds of mathematicians down through the ages until it was shown to be impossible by P. L. Wantzel in 1837. However, ingenious mechanical devices have been devised to produce the required trisection.

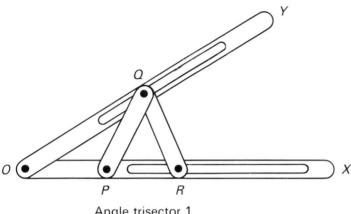

Angle trisector 1

One device consists of two bars OX and OY, pivoted at O, and linked by two bars PQ and RQ as shown in angle trisector 1. $OP = PQ = RQ$, with PQ pivoting about P, and Q and R able to slide along OY and OX respectively. Using the properties of an isosceles triangle and the angle sum of a triangle, it is easy to show that angle YOX is always one-third of angle YQR.

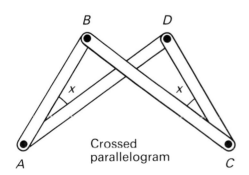

Crossed parallelogram

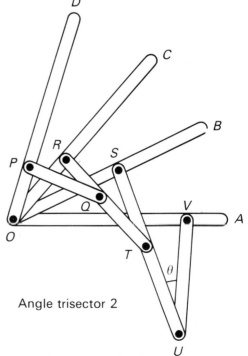

Angle trisector 2

The second device is based on crossed parallelograms such as $ABCD$ where the four rods AB, BC, CD and DA are free to pivot about their ends, and $AB = CD$, $AD = BC$. When crossed as shown the angle BAD is always equal to angle BCD. In the angle trisector 2, the rods OA, OB, OC, OD will always move so that angle AOB = angle BOC = angle COD, because their movement is constrained by three similar crossed parallelograms, namely $OPQR$, $ORTS$ and $OSUV$. Find all the other angles in the linkage equal to θ to see why it works.

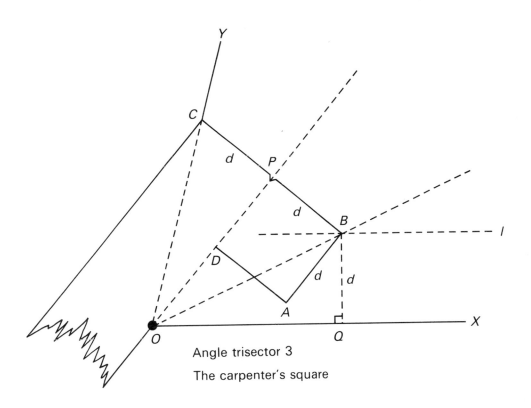

Angle trisector 3

The carpenter's square

The third device is simply a carpenter's square such that $AB = AD = BP = CP = d$, so that $DABP$ is a square. To trisect any angle XOY, first draw line l parallel to OX, a distance d from OX, using the parallel sides of the square. Then slide the square so that its edge always passes through O, and B is on l, until C coincides with OY. It is not difficult to see why OCP is congruent to OBP, which in turn is congruent to OBQ, so angle COP = angle BOP = angle BOQ.

To really appreciate these devices make models of them using card strips and paper fasteners.

140 Rational approximations to $\sqrt{N}$

If we want to find the square root of a number we usually make use of the $\sqrt{}$ key on our calculator and are not too concerned as to how the result is found. But suppose you did not have a calculator to hand, then what follows are two methods which can quite quickly enable you to obtain as accurate an approximation to the square root of a number as you could wish.

Consider the mapping

$$\frac{a}{b} \to \frac{a + 2b}{a + b}$$

Taking $a = b = 1$ to start, and carrying out this mapping repeatedly on each new rational number formed, after nine steps we have the following sequence:

$$\frac{1}{1} \quad \frac{3}{2} \quad \frac{7}{5} \quad \frac{17}{12} \quad \frac{41}{29} \quad \frac{99}{70} \quad \frac{239}{169} \quad \frac{577}{408} \quad \frac{1393}{985} \quad \frac{3363}{2378}$$

Now $\frac{239}{169} = 1.4142$, which is a good approximation to $\sqrt{2}$, while $\frac{3363}{2378} = 1.4142136$ is accurate to 8 significant figures!

To simplify the calculations the initial values were both taken as 1, but, amazingly, a and b could have been any non-zero numbers and the sequence would still have converged onto $\sqrt{2}$.

More generally, the mapping

$$\frac{a}{b} \to \frac{a + Nb}{a + b}$$

will generate a sequence converging on $\sqrt{N}$.

Try some special cases and see how rapidly the sequences converge.

To see why the sequences converge to N, in the limit

$$\frac{a}{b} = \frac{a + Nb}{a + b} = \frac{a/b + N}{a/b + 1}$$

Put $\frac{a}{b} = L$, then $\qquad L = \frac{(L + N)}{(L + 1)}$

from which $\qquad L^2 = N$

The second method is one attributed to Hero, an Ancient Greek mathematician. In this case a sequence of numbers is generated from the mapping

$$a \to \frac{1}{2}\left(a + \frac{N}{a}\right)$$

a can be any non-zero number but is usually chosen as a reasonable first approximation to $\sqrt{N}$.

Suppose $N = 5$, then taking $a = 2$ is a good starting point and the mapping produces

$$2 \quad \frac{9}{4} \quad \frac{161}{72} \quad \frac{51\,841}{23\,184}$$

Now $\frac{161}{72} = 2.236\,111$, while $\frac{51\,841}{23\,184} = 2.236\,068$, which already compares with $2.236\,068$ on my calculator. In other words, this sequence converges very rapidly. In very rough terms the number of significant figures doubles at each stage!

One way of seeing why this method works is to appreciate that if a is less than $\sqrt{N}$, then N/a is greater than $\sqrt{N}$, so their average must lie between them.

141 Artificial gravity

We are used to seeing science fiction films or television programmes with people walking about normally in spaceships without question. In practice, if people are to spend long periods in space it will be necessary to create artificial gravity so that people feel the same weight as they would on Earth.

But how? One of the most realistic solutions for an orbiting space station would be to design it as a large wheel. The tube around the outside would form a torus in which the people would spend most of their time, and the artificial gravity would be created by spinning the wheel about its axis.

Where would the floor of the tube be?

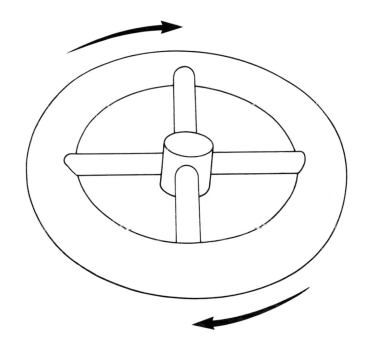

142 Taking Mansfield for a walk

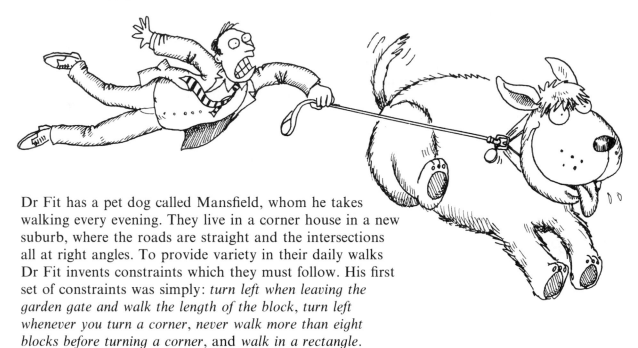

Dr Fit has a pet dog called Mansfield, whom he takes walking every evening. They live in a corner house in a new suburb, where the roads are straight and the intersections all at right angles. To provide variety in their daily walks Dr Fit invents constraints which they must follow. His first set of constraints was simply: *turn left when leaving the garden gate and walk the length of the block*, *turn left whenever you turn a corner*, *never walk more than eight blocks before turning a corner*, and *walk in a rectangle*.

Such a set of constraints limited them to rectangular routes, but allowed a considerable variety, and on New Year's Day 1988 Dr Fit made a New Year's resolution to take Mansfield on a different route each day, starting that very evening, until every possible route had been completed.

On what date did they accomplish their feat?

Feeling fit after so much walking, Dr Fit decided to modify the constraints so that more walks were possible, by *leaving out the condition that the route was to be a rectangle*, but adding the constraint that, *having left home they should not turn left more than five times*.

When they had completed all the new routes Dr Fit presented Mansfield with a smart new collar to celebrate the occasion.

What was the date?

Exhilarated by this fine achievement, Dr Fit decided to change his constraints once more to include the possibility of *any number of left turns*. But he also added the constraint that *no part of the path should be retraced on a particular walk*.

On what date did Dr Fit and Mansfield celebrate the achievement of completing all the new walks available to them?

76

COMMENTARY

1 A fabulous family!

Great Grandmother Bountiful was 85. She had 5 daughters, 20 grandsons and 60 great-granddaughters.

2 Damage limitation!

Only one link needs to be cut. If, after the first race, the jeweller removes the third link, the chain will have been divided into three pieces containing one, two and four links respectively.

By using suitable exchange of these pieces with the jeweller, Fred will be able to match all his commitments.

3 Primeval instincts!

One solution is given here, but it is not unique.

$$\begin{array}{r} 2794 \\ +\ 3790 \\ \hline 6584 \end{array}$$

4 Spatial perception

5 Spawning coins!

Put 3 on 4, 6 on 7, 9 on 10, 12 on 1. Clearly this is not a unique solution; removing one coin from each side to put on a different corner would give the required result.

6 Think again!

Yes! For example,

$$\frac{-2}{3} = \frac{2}{-3}$$

7 Matchstick machinations!

(a)

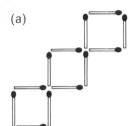 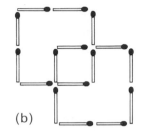 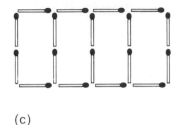

(b)

(c)

8 Keep off my line!

A maximum of six counters can be placed on the board.

This problem is equivalent to the chess problem of placing six queens on a 6 × 6 board so that no queen is attacking or being attacked by any other. It could be used as the basis of an interesting game of strategy, where two players take it in turns to add a counter to the board until one player is unable to play without putting a counter on a line already occupied.

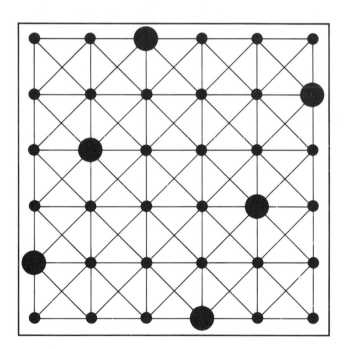

9 Printing the parish magazine

2	15
4	13

16	1
14	3

6	11
8	9

12	5
10	7

10 Maximise the product

The largest product is formed from 9642×87531.

A neat strategy in solving this and similar problems is to start with the highest digits at the front, alternating between the numbers and at the same time keeping the final numbers as close together in size as possible. Compare this with having a rectangle, the lengths of whose sides are equal to your numbers and whose area you are trying to maximise. The closer to a square you can make it with a given perimeter, the larger the area.

11 Honey bears' picnic!

Here is one solution, suggested by Nick Chatrath from Orpington in Kent, England. Can you find a more efficient one?

The columns correspond to the four containers and their contents after each pouring of honey from one of them into one or more other containers.

21	*11*	*8*	*5*
21	0	0	0
10	11	0	0
10	6	0	5
10	0	6	5
10	5	6	0
10	5	1	5
10	10	1	0
10	10	0	1
2	10	8	1
2	11	7	1
2	7	7	5
7	7	7	0

12 Can you do better?

The second solution here gives 1 to 43 but may not be the best.

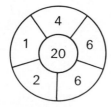
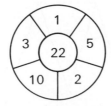

14 Arboreal alignments!

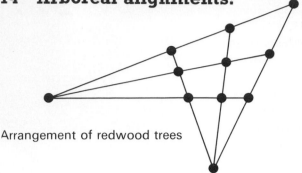

Arrangement of redwood trees

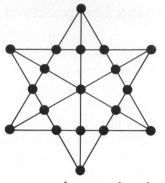

Arrangement of copper-beech trees

16 The Japanese water garden

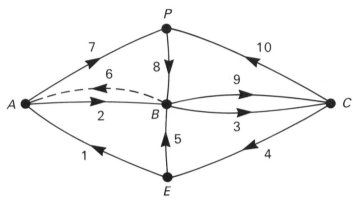

The garden is equivalent to the network shown, where the arcs represent the bridges and stepping stones. As it stands the network has four odd nodes, but to be able to design a route which starts at E and ends at P, having traversed each arc once, requires that all the nodes are even except E and P. This is achieved by building a second bridge between islands A and B. Then one solution is to cross the bridges and stepping stones in the order indicated by the numbers on the arcs.

17 Mental gymnastics!

$70 \times 148 = 35 \times 296$

18 An isosceles dissection

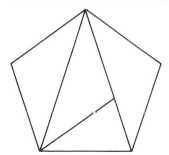
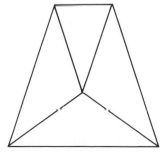

19 Domino magic

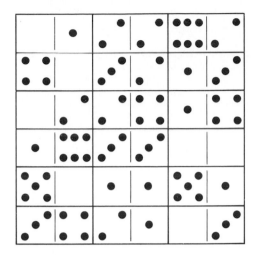

20 The meal track

The shortest distance is approximately 32 ft. It is achieved by first going down the side wall at an angle, meeting the floor 8 ft from *E*, and then travelling across the floor to *G*.

$$AG^2 = (25^2 + 20^2) = 1025$$

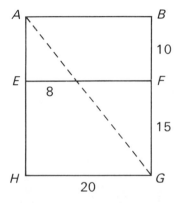

21 The time trial

His task is impossible. He has used up all the available time on the outward journey, so no speed would be fast enough.

22 Together in threes

```
B → BANK       WEB        BOIL
R →  CAR       IRENE      ROWS
T →  TAIL      STEM       KNOT
  I↗  ↑          ↑          ↑  ↖N
     A           E          O
```

Six words will need to be moved to obtain the array as shown, where the common letters are indicated. The words were carefully chosen so that no other array is possible.

23 Symmetric years

It is a fairly rare occurrence for a symmetric number to have all its prime factors symmetric too. For example,

$1881 = 11 \times 171$, but $171 = 3 \times 3 \times 19$.

The only years since 1000 to the present are:

$1111 = 11 \times 101$
$1331 = 11 \times 11 \times 11$
$1441 = 11 \times 131$
$1661 = 11 \times 151$

The only future years before the year 3000 are

$2112 = 2 \times 2 \times 2 \times 2 \times 2 \times 2 \times 3 \times 11$
$2222 = 2 \times 11 \times 101$
$2662 = 2 \times 11 \times 11 \times 11$
$2772 = 2 \times 2 \times 3 \times 3 \times 7 \times 11$
$2882 = 2 \times 11 \times 131$

So it really is a once-in-a-lifetime experience!

24 A circuitous guard inspection

The solution is not unique; two possible solutions are shown here. If the diameters of the circular paths are 100 m, 200 m and 300 m, what is the shortest route possible?

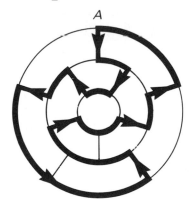 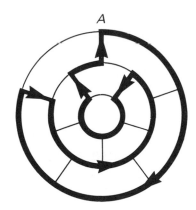

25 Crossing the lakes

C and D cross together. C returns leaving D.
A crosses and D returns, leaving A.
C and D cross together. C returns leaving A and D.
B crosses and D returns.
C and D cross together. C returns leaving A, B and D.
C crosses with the rucksacks.

26 Know the time!

Twice. 6 o'clock in the morning and in the evening, unless you are thinking of a 24-hour clock when it will only occur at 1200 hours.

28 Pinball pursuits

Routes are shown here which maximise the score, but they are not necessarily unique.

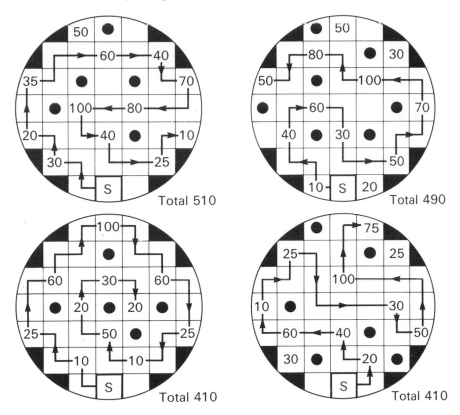

Total 510

Total 490

Total 410

Total 410

29 Happy numbers!

Twenty numbers in the range from 1 to 100 are happy, and they may be presented in a tree diagram showing the chain of numbers which takes them to 1.

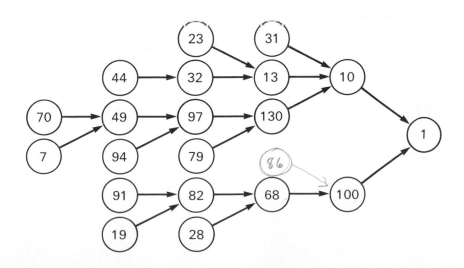

Clearly, any number along the chain linking a happy number to 1 will also be happy. New numbers may be found by trial and error or by systematically working backwards from a happy number by finding a set of digits whose square will sum to it. For example, 176 is a happy number and

$$9^2 + 8^2 + 5^2 + 2^2 + 1^2 + 1^2 = 176$$

so any number formed from the six digits 9, 8, 5, 2, 1, 1, such as 129 851, will be happy. It should also be clear that any permutation of the digits of a happy number will be happy; in addition, introducing zeros into a happy number gives another happy number. So from 176 we can, for example, generate 617 or 70 160 or 7 100 006.

Sad numbers have no fixed end point but travel endlessly round the same cycle of eight numbers (4, 16, 37, 58, 89, 145, 42, 20) then back to 4.

For example, $1276 \rightarrow 90 \rightarrow 81 \rightarrow 65 \rightarrow 61 \rightarrow 37$ (one of the cycle), from which point on it continues to circle as shown.

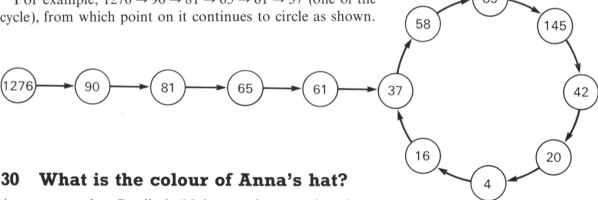

30 What is the colour of Anna's hat?

Anna argues that Candice's 'No' can only mean that she cannot see two blue hats in front of her, for otherwise Candice would have been able to deduce immediately that her hat was red. Betty would also have made this deduction from Candice's reply, so if she was looking at a blue hat in front of her she would have known that she herself was wearing a red hat. As she was not able to determine the colour of her own hat, it follows that Betty must have been looking at a red hat on Anna's head.

31 Cubical contortions!

Surriya has 64 bricks.

$$64 = 8 \times 8 = 4 \times 4 \times 4$$

Graham has 89 bricks.

$$89 = 8 \times 8 + 4 \times 4 + 3 \times 3$$
$$= 7 \times 7 + 6 \times 6 + 2 \times 2$$
$$= 8 \times 8 + 5 \times 5$$

32 Empty the glass!

This puzzle can be quite frustrating, but satisfying to solve.

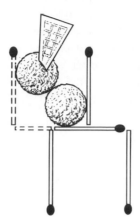

33 · Mum's happy!

The only number which is square, happy (see activity 29 for the definition of a happy number) and in an acceptable age range is 49.

34 A fascinating pentagonal array!

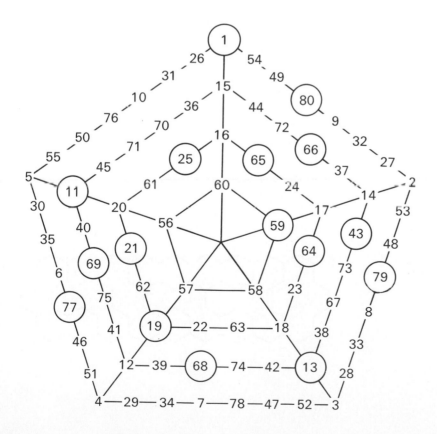

35 Bending Euclid!

Take, for example, the lines of longitude corresponding to 0° and 90°, and the equator. These intersect in a triangle whose angles are all 90°. On a spherical surface the shortest distance between two points is always part of a great circle, so in this sense the great circles play the same role as straight lines in a plane. On a sphere, triangles formed from these circles can have an angle sum anywhere between 180° and 360°. Investigate!

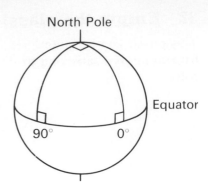

36 Tetrahexagons

The seven shapes are often given names as shown in the diagram. Solutions to the bunch of grapes and the tower are not unique. One of each is shown here in case you thought the task impossible!

Propeller

Arch

Pistol

Bee

Worm

Bar

Wave

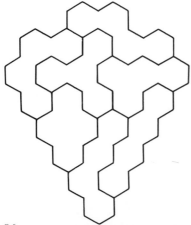

37 Bowler of the match?

In the first innings Macartney has an average of 21.5, against 32 for Noble. Also Macartney does better in the second innings with an average of 1.5 compared to Noble's 3.5. But don't jump to hasty conclusions for, taking both innings together, Macartney has taken 6 wickets for 49 runs at an average of approximately 8.2, while Noble has taken 7 wickets for 53 at the better average of about 7.6. Noble also took more wickets, so undoubtedly he should get the award!

38 Knight's tours!

With both the Japanese lady and the furniture lorry a re-entrant tour is possible, so a route can be achieved by starting at any square. However, the other shape is only traceable if the route starts at particular squares. The solutions given may not be unique. Try creating shapes of your own on which it is possible to trace out a knight's tour.

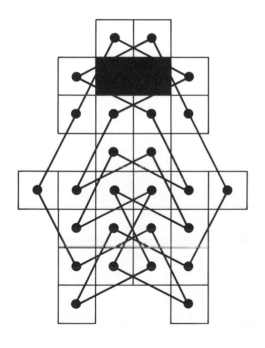

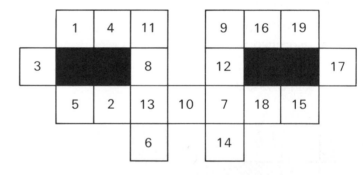

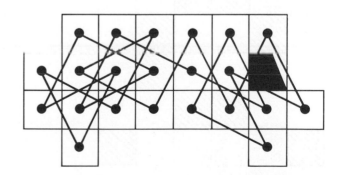

39 Ornithology!

These are some of the possible solutions.

707	121	303
+ 8 249	+ 5 803	+ 5 618
21 309	86 923	64 708
30 265	92 847	70 629

40 Skimming across the river!

In theory an infinite number would be required! But most of the bounces would be so small as to be imperceptible, and the total number of bounces would not take an infinite time, so Peter's task is not impossible.

41 Digital dance!

142 857. You may recognise it as the recurring sequence of digits associated with division by 7.

42 Two's enough!

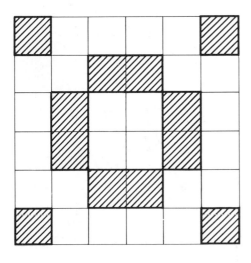
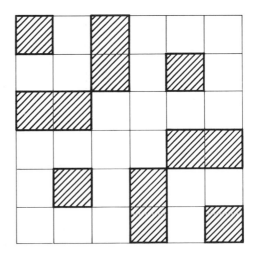

43   A pentomino game

This game was invented by Solomon Golomb, the author of
the book *Polyominoes* (George Allen and Unwin), which
has created such a widespread interest in these shapes. It is
interesting to play the game on other-size boards and to
devise winning strategies. An interesting problem related to
this is to determine the smallest number of pieces which
could be placed on an $m \times n$ board so that no space
remains capable of accepting any of the remaining pieces.
Minimal solutions for a 6×6 and a 7×7 board are shown
here. They are not unique.

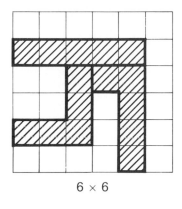

6 × 6

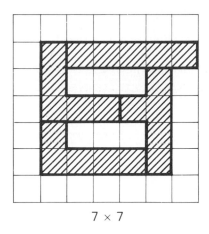

7 × 7

47   The windmill

Many puzzles of this type are
to be found in *The Domino
Book* by Fredrick Berndt
(Bantam Books).

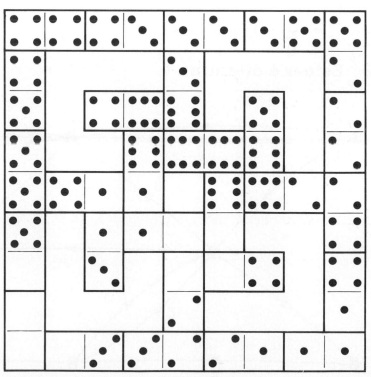

48 Prime addresses!

Professor Newton was at No. 73 and Dr Lagrange was at
No. 83. Their ages are 63 and 73 respectively.

$$73 = 8^2 + 3^2$$

49 Exercising Bouncer!

Matt and Lina are approaching each other at a speed of
8 km per hour, so meet up in half an hour, in which time
Bouncer will have covered 15 km!

50 An ancient riddle

He was $31\frac{1}{2}$ and she was $34\frac{1}{2}$.

51 Double glazed!

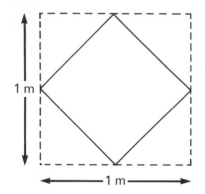

52 Esther's dilemma

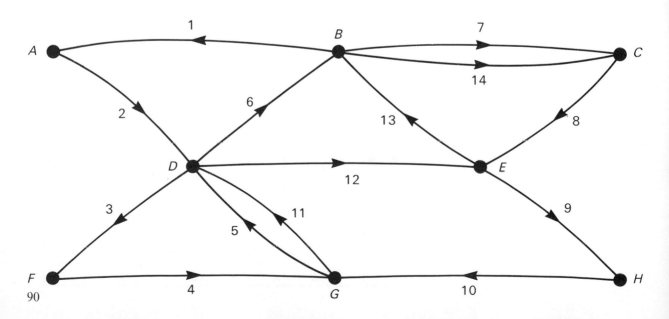

The problem is best tackled by replacing each room by a node, and drawing arcs connecting nodes corresponding to each doorway as shown. The problem is then reduced to seeing whether or not the network is traversable. Now all the nodes are even except *B* and *C*, so solutions are possible as long as they start at *B* and end at *C*, or vice versa. One such solution starts at *B* and follows the arcs (doorways) as numbered, ending at *C*. But no solution is possible which starts and ends in the same room, although this would be made possible by making another doorway between *B* and *C*, or blocking off one of the existing ones, for the effect of this on the network would be to make all the nodes even.

54 Piling up the ancestors!

The argument given ignores the fact that many ancestors will be in common. For example, your parents might share a common great-grandfather. In fact the impossibility of this very large number of ancestors means the argument can be used to show that everyone has common ancestors.

55 Equal shares for all!

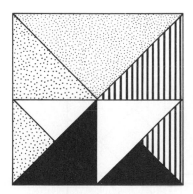

56 Coincident birthdays!

Luke is 17, Mark is 51 and Matthew is 102.

This puzzle is based on the realisation that if two integers m and n differ by a prime number p, then $m + r$ and $n + r$ only have a common factor at intervals of length p.

57 Tetraboloes

The 14 different possible tetraboloes are shown here, together with a solution for each of the squares. The solutions are not unique. Many other shapes can be made, of course, using the tetraboloes, and one investigation you might like to try is to see how many different sizes of rectangle you can make. Interestingly, no rectangle exists which uses all 14 of the tetraboloes. For a discussion of this last point a good reference is *Mathematical Magic Show* by Martin Gardner (Penguin).

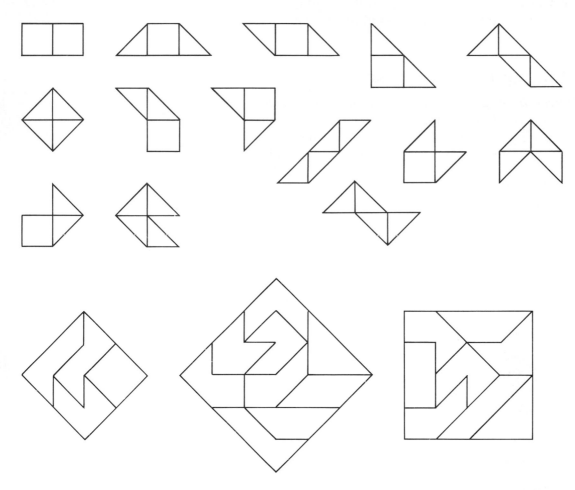

58 Symbolism!

(*a*) XIX, take away I leaves XX.

(*b*) A three-digit number is only divisible by 9 if its digit sum is a multiple of 9. $8 + 6 + 1 = 15$, so you may think there are no ways. However, the 6 symbol inverted gives a 9, and makes possible 981, 918, 891, 819, 198, 189!

59 Find the missing money!

What £2? The friends have only paid £27 (not £30), which
was £1 more than the correct bill of £26, and this is in the
waiter's pocket! Ironically, the friends were so impressed
with the waiter's 'honesty' that, on leaving, they each left
him £1 as a tip!

60 Manipulating calendar digits

Restricting the range of mathematical symbols makes the
task more challenging, but at the same time more
accessible. The solutions which caused me the most
problems were:

$$40 = ((9 \times 9) - 1)/2$$
$$42 = (9/0.2 - \sqrt{9}) \times 1$$
$$44 = 9(\sqrt{9} + 2) - 1$$

How about trying for the century with the four digits
corresponding to the year of your birth?

61 The square pack

Put four of the squares on top of one another and cut
through them from one corner to the middle of an opposite
edge. Then arrange the pieces as shown to form the large
square.

cut

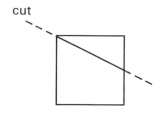
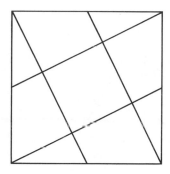

62 The hangover!

There are two possible ways of dividing the remaining
bottles to ensure that each student has their fair share of $3\frac{1}{2}$
bottles:

$1\ 1\ 1\frac{1}{2}0000 \qquad 1\ 1\ 1\frac{1}{2}0000$

$1\ 1\frac{1}{2}\frac{1}{2}\frac{1}{2}000 \quad \text{or} \quad 1\ 1\ 1\frac{1}{2}0000$

$1\ 1\frac{1}{2}\frac{1}{2}\frac{1}{2}000 \qquad 1\frac{1}{2}\frac{1}{2}\frac{1}{2}\frac{1}{2}\frac{1}{2}00$

63 Extrapolating from five seconds!

(a) Eleven seconds

(b) Five ladybirds

64 Three square units

Solutions are not possible if you try to keep to rectangular polygons, but once you allow your thinking to incorporate other angles than right-angles then an infinity of solutions can be found. Three are shown to give a stimulus to your further endeavours!

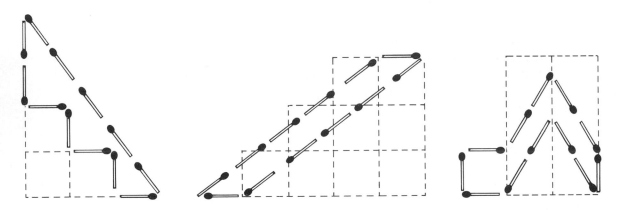

65 Magic tetrahedra

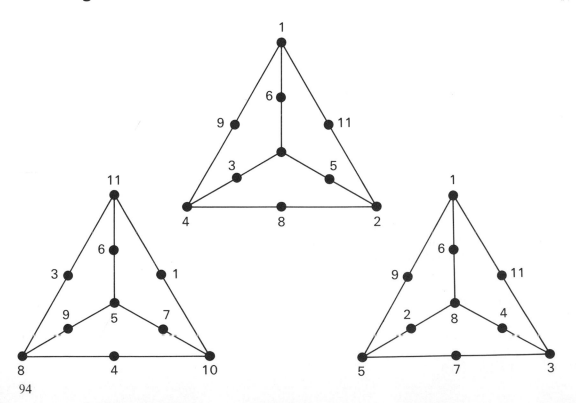

Three solutions are shown, with the tetrahedra viewed from above. They indicate ways in which different solutions may be generated from any solution already found. The left-hand solution is produced from the middle one by using the transformation $n \rightarrow 12 - n$, on each number. The right-hand solution is obtained by considering just one triangular face of the tetrahedron in the middle (the lower triangle in this case) and interchanging the vertex numbers with those in the middle of the opposite edge. As a tetrahedron has four faces this last device generates four new solutions from the starting one. These two devices together enable ten different solutions to be generated from any given one. I believe there are only 20 solutions in all, which are linked together by the above transformations into two independent sets. Let me know if you find any more! These solutions are summarised below by giving the magic total and the numbers at the vertices.

Magic total	Vertex numbers			
14	(1, 2, 3, 5)	(1, 2, 3, 7)	(1, 2, 4, 7)	
15	(1, 3, 4, 5)	(1, 3, 5, 8)		
16	(2, 3, 6, 9)	(1, 4, 5, 9)		
17	(2, 4, 6, 10)			
18	(4, 5, 6, 11)	(1, 6, 7, 8)	(1, 6, 7, 9)	(3, 5, 6, 11)
19	(2, 6, 8, 10)			
20	(3, 7, 8, 11)	(3, 6, 9, 10)		
21	(4, 7, 9, 11)	(7, 8, 9, 11)		
22	(5, 8, 10, 11)	(5, 9, 10, 11)	(7, 9, 10, 11)	

No solution is possible with the numbers from 1 to 10 as they consist of five odd numbers and five even numbers. A little experimenting will soon convince you that such a distribution of odds and evens will not enable you to obtain either an odd magic total or an even magic total.

66 Fault-free rectangles

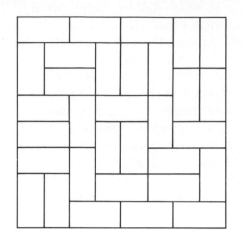

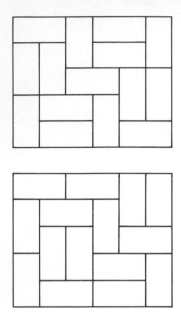

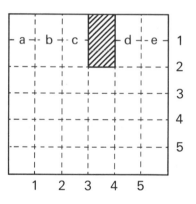

The smallest fault-free rectangle is a 6 × 5, for which two solutions are given here. The smallest such square is the 8 × 8, also shown. Clearly, the 5 × 5 and 7 × 7 squares cannot even be made as their areas are an odd number of unit squares, but it might have seemed that a solution to the 6 × 6 square would be found, given enough patience. However, there is a neat proof that no such fault-free solution exists.

A 6 × 6 square has potentially ten fault lines, five vertical and five horizontal. To block one of these lines a block must cross it, so as there are ten lines a fault-free solution would require ten blocks to cross them. Now it takes (6 × 6) ÷ 2 = 18 blocks to cover the square, so some of the lines might be crossed by more than one block, but at least one line could only be covered by one block. Suppose line 1 is crossed by just one block, as shown. Then there are five spaces (a, b, c, d, e) on the line beside it which are all to be covered by blocks lying horizontally. But this is impossible no matter where we put the single block which crosses the line. Hence no fault-free solution is possible.

67 Dr Shah in the country

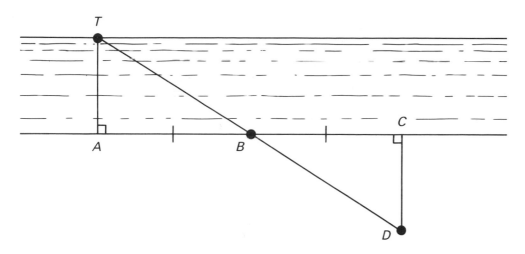

Ravi walks along the river bank to a point *A* (see diagram), from where he can see a tree, *T*, (or another easily identified object) on the bank immediately opposite. He then walks along the bank, counting his steps, to a point *B*. He has his aunt stand at *B*, while he continues along the bank an equal number of steps to *C*. Then, turning with his back to the river, he walks inland to the point *D* where *T*, *B*, and *D* are in a straight line. Triangles *TAB* and *DCB* are now congruent, so *CD* is equal to the width of the river, *AT*. How far Ravi walks from *A* to *B* is theoretically not significant, but the best result would, in practice, be obtained when *AB* was approximately equal to *AT*.

68 In their prime

Mrs Babbage was born in 1938, Mr Babbage in 1940 and Rachel in 1970.

The only numbers expressible in the given form corresponding to their possible ages, are:

 24 40 54 56 88 104

Given the fact that they met when both were at school, the parents' ages must be 54 and 56. The fact that Rachel was the youngest daughter rules out the likelihood of her being 40, for her mother would then have been 16, so Rachel must be 24.

The germ of the idea for this puzzle was given to me by Joe Gilks of Deakin University, Australia.

69 Which way to Birminster's spire?

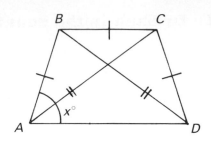

Birminster's spire is on a bearing of 018° from Ablethorpe's. The spires are in fact positioned at four of the vertices of a regular pentagon.

Consider the diagram shown, based on the given information. Triangles ABC and BCD are both isosceles and congruent, as are triangles ACD and DBA. Let angle $BAD = x°$, then angles ABD, ACD, and ADC will also be $x°$. Using the angle sum of triangle ACD gives angle $CAD = 180° - 2x°$, hence angle $BAC = 3x° - 180°$. Considering the interior angles of triangle ABC, we get

$$180 = (3x - 180) + x + (3x - 180) + (3x - 180)$$

from which $x = 72$, and hence the bearing from North of 018°.

70 Unit fractions

The fact that x cannot be smaller than 6 or larger than 14 limits the search. When $x = 6$, there are thirteen distinct solutions and the corresponding values of x, y, z are given.

x	y	z	x	y	z
6	31	930	6	40	120
6	32	480	6	42	105
6	33	330	6	45	90
6	34	255	6	48	80
6	35	210	6	50	75
6	36	180	6	55	66
6	39	130			

When $x = 7$ there are only four solutions, and when $x = 8$ there are five solutions. What was the largest value of x for which you were able to find a solution?

To find solutions, for example where $x = 6$, we have

$$\frac{1}{5} = \frac{1}{6} + \frac{1}{y} + \frac{1}{z}$$

from which we can obtain the relation

$$(y - 30)z = 30y$$

and then systematically look for integer solutions for z as we let y take integer values starting with $y = 31$.

71 Paper tearing!

Suppose, for argument's sake, we let the paper be one hundredth of a centimetre thick. Then, after 40 tearings, the pile would have 2^{40} pieces in it and be 0.01×2^{40} cm high. Now 2^{40} is approximately 1.1×10^{12}, so the height of the pile of paper would be about

$$0.01 \times 1.1 \times 10^{12}\,\text{cm}$$
$$= 1.1 \times 10^{8}\,\text{m}$$
$$= 110\,000\,\text{km}$$

72 A devilish domino distribution!

There is only one solution to the placement of the uncovered squares, as you can see from the diagram. But then the dominoes can be placed in many ways. Readers may well have spotted the connection with the problem of placing eight pawns on a chess board so that no three of them are in a straight line.

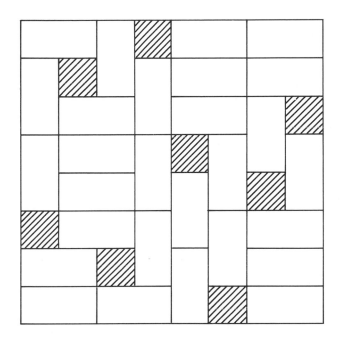

73 Tri-hex

This game was invented by Thomas O'Beirne of Glasgow, who discussed strategies for playing it in the *New Scientist* (11 January 1962). If the first counter is placed on one of the interior circles of the outside triangle and the first player than plays to force the second player's next move, the game should always be won by the player who started.

74 Mr Mailshot's muddle

Mr Mailshot will only need to have a look at one ball to be able to decide how to readdress the package. He must open the parcel wrongly addressed to Miss Clapham and open one box. If he sees a red crystal ball then he knows that this parcel must be the one for Mrs Ambridge. It follows that, as every parcel was wrongly addressed, the one addressed to Mrs Ambridge should go to Mr Beaufort, and the one addressed to Mr Beaufort should go to Miss Clapham. A similar analysis follows if the ball was found to be blue.

75 Staggering!

Nothing! Joe's original argument was false. Assuming the lane width d is the same for both tracks, then the stagger required between adjacent lanes for a race of one lap is $2\pi d$, so if the 400 m race on the 200 m track had been run throughout in lanes the stagger would have needed to be $4\pi d$. Luckily for Joe only the first lap was in lanes so his stagger was correct. A case of two wrongs make a right!

76 The queen's pursuit

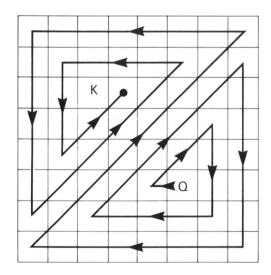

77 Ageing!

Let m be the number of the birth month, let d be the day of the month, and a be the age. Then the steps, if carried out correctly, compute $10\,000m + 100d + a + 11\,111$.

78 Follow my leader?

They could have been on opposite sides of the North Pole, both travelling south, away from each other, at 3 mph. But more generally, if they start 10 miles apart on different lines of longitude near the North Pole and travel south their paths will diverge rapidly. In these cases, and similar ones near the South Pole travelling north, the likely mode of transport would be on skis. But, recognising that two lines of longitude diverge from each other all the way from a pole to the Equator, two pilots of jet planes far from a pole but travelling south or north towards the Equator could satisfy the conditions of this puzzle.

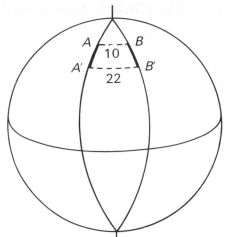

79 The disappearing act!

The flaw in the argument is in the assumption that the rectangle is 9 units long. Triangle C is not isosceles. It is 1 unit high but its hypotenuse is not at 45°, and its base is of length $\frac{8}{7}$ units. Hence the rectangle is $\frac{64}{7}$ units long, giving it an area of 64 square units.

80 The missing digit!

This trick depends on the fact that (a) any number minus its digits is divisible by 9, and (b) for a number to be divisible by 9 its digits sum must be divisible by 9.

So, when your friend gives you all but one of the digits, you add them together and the missing digit will be the digit required to add to the total to make it divisible by 9. In the example given, $2 + 9 + 3 = 14$, so 4 is required to bring it to 18, the next multiple of 9.

Now can you prove the two properties of numbers, base 10, on which the trick depends?

81 Romantic?

SIX	IX	XL
− IX	X	L
S	I	X

82 Mustafa's pride and joy!

The oracle has cheated.

$\frac{1}{2} + \frac{1}{4} + \frac{1}{6} = \frac{11}{12}$, but as Chief Mustafa had not made it known who was to have the remaining $\frac{1}{12}$ of his oxen, the oracle had shared it between the sons so they all ended up with more than their 'fair' share, confused but happy.

83 Common factors

Only one solution apart from reflections and rotations is possible.

These numbers can be used as the basis of a game similar to noughts and crosses. Write each of the nine numbers on a separate card. Put the cards on the table, face up, and invite two players to take it in turn to select a card. The first player to hold three cards with a common factor wins.

	2	7	5	17	3
	↘	↓	↓	↓	↙
19 →		266	95	969	
11 →		77	330	187	
13 →		273	65	442	

84 Fill the gap!

The missing number is 81.

Each segment on the left-hand side is related to the one diagonally opposite on the right-hand side. Each number can be expressed as a power of a lower number; both the base and the index of the right-hand number is incremented by 1 to give the left-hand number, for example $4^3 \rightarrow 5^4$. Although most of the numbers can be expressed as different powers, the 8, which is required to give the missing number, can only be expressed as 2^3, thus giving the solution as 3^4.

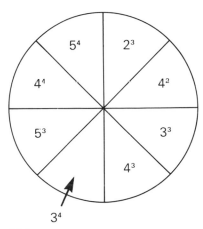

102

87   Joe Joiner's new bench

The bench top is 210 cm by 60 cm.

Joe cut 60 cm off the 270 cm plank and joined it, end on, to the 150 cm plank to give himself three planks of length 210 cm. He then cut the 180 cm plank into three pieces of length 60 cm to form the battens.

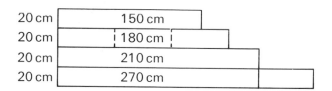

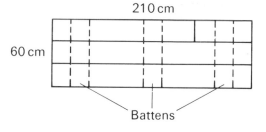

88   Partitioning the plantation

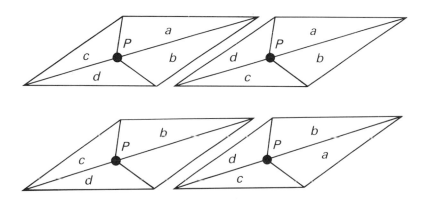

The common corner P must lie on a diagonal of the parallelogram and divide it in the ratio $2:3$. Hence there are four possible positions for the common corner. In each of the positions for P there are then four ways of allocating the plots, so in all there are 16 different possible allocations.

89   When was Professor Danzig born?

She was born on 27 September 1951.

This follows from the fact that $11\,111 = 41 \times 271$, so she must have been 41 on the 271st day of 1992. Did you forget that 1992 was a leap year?

90   This number is unique!

$69^2 = 4761$ $69^3 = 328\,509$

91 Triangular animals!

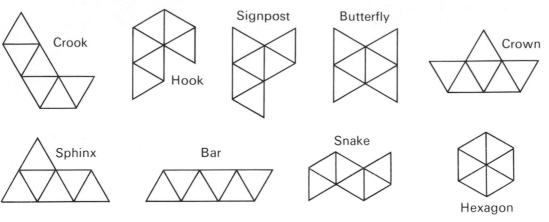

There are twelve different triangular animals using six tiles. They are shown together with the names used to identify them.

Many solutions are possible for the diamond and hexagon. The two shown for the hexagon were sent to me by Yoshio Kimura from Kobe, Japan, and both leave out the lobster, the signpost and the crown.

No solution to the hexagon is possible which uses the sphinx unless the yacht is also used. Why?

An excellent reference on all puzzles of this type is *Polyominoes* by Solomon W. Golomb (George Allen and Unwin).

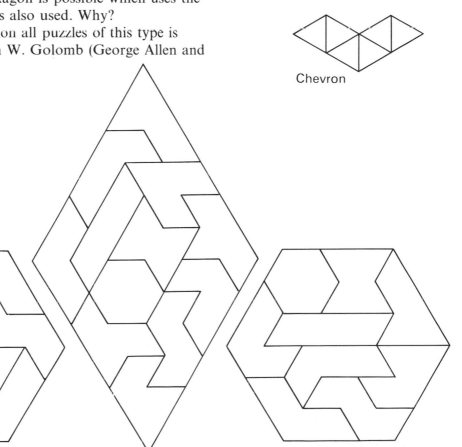

93 Adventure holidays!

A case of playing around with Pythagorean triples where one of the numbers is 12.

$$AC = 20, \qquad CB = 13, \qquad AB = 21$$

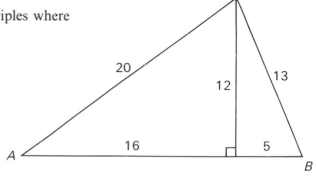

94 Cross out nine digits

Here are three solutions.

1̶11	111	1̶1̶1̶
333	3̶3̶3	3̶3̶3
5̶5̶5	5̶5̶5	5̶5̶5
777	777	̶777
9̶9̶9	999	999

1111   1111   1111

95 A sequential challenge

The solution is not unique. One solution is:

7   18   13   1   16   5   14   4   20   6   19   12

The longest sequence possible contains sixteen integers and an example of such a sequence using 1 to 16 is:

10   6   12   9   13   2   11   1   16   7   15   3   8   4   14   5

The best way to verify that such a sequence does not contain a sub-sequence of five increasing or decreasing numbers is to represent them graphically as shown.

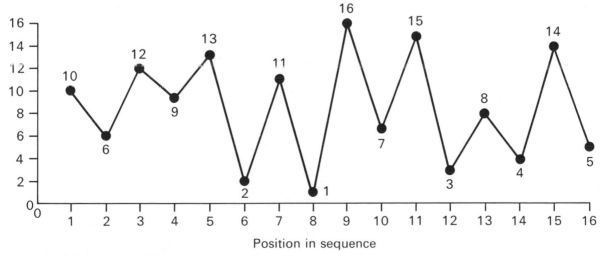

Position in sequence

But the neatest such solution is:

13   14   15   16   9   10   11   12   5   6   7   8   1   2   3   4

96 Fencing!

Whatever the slopes, the number of panels depends only on the horizontal distance between A and C, as panels are fixed vertically and are stepped down the slopes.

Pythagoras' theorem gives the horizontal distance as:

$$\sqrt{(90^2 - 54^2)} + \sqrt{(78^2 - 30^2)} = 144\,\text{m}$$

Hence only 72 panels are required.

97 Triangular Nim

Winning strategies can be developed. Clearly any player who leaves 11111 or 111 in the rows must win. Further, if any player who leaves 22 (that is, two rows of 2 coins) can force a win. If their opponent removes 2, they remove 1 from the remaining row leaving their opponent to take the last coin. If, on the other hand, their opponent takes 1, leaving 12, they can remove the 2, again forcing a win.

See *The Amazing Mathematical Amusement Arcade* by the author (Cambridge University Press) for a more detailed analysis of winning strategies for Nim.

98 Bridge that gap!

Let one plank rest with each of its ends just touching the perimeter of the pond as shown in the diagram. Then, by Pythagoras' theorem, the distance from the plank's centre to the middle of the pond is

$$\sqrt{(20^2 - (4.9/2)^2)} = 19.849\,\text{m}$$

to 3 decimal places. So the second plank, with one end on the middle of this plank, could stretch more than 5 m towards the pond's centre and thus reach the island.

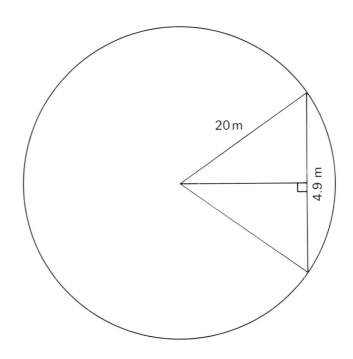

99 Custom control!

36 officers would need to be deployed at bridges a, e, f, h, m and n.

100 Magic!

The following solution is thought to be unique, apart from reversing the order:

  8 10 1 3 2 7 8

101 Save the farmer's legs!

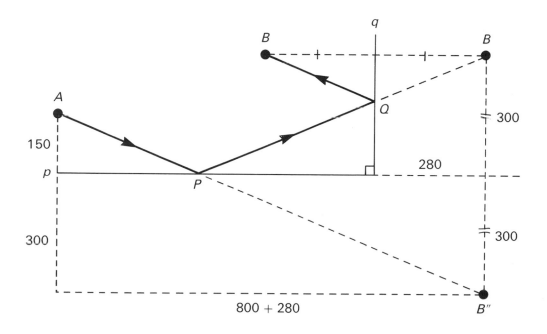

The shortest route is the path which makes equal angles with p and equal angles with q. It can be found by first taking the reflection of B in q to give B', then the reflection of B' in the extension of p to give B''. If the farmer walked towards B'' until meeting fence p, and then towards B' until meeting q, and finally to B, his route would be the optimum. Consideration of the diagram shows that

$$AP + PQ + QB = AP + PQ + QB'$$
$$= AP + PB''$$
$$= AB''$$

Then $(AB'')^2 = (150 + 300)^2 + (800 + 280)^2$

from which $AB'' = 1170\,\text{m}$

102 Quadrupled!

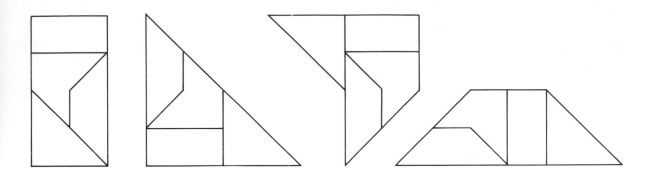

103 A painless deduction!

The sum of the digits 1, 2, 3, 4, . . . 9 is 45.
Now $987\,654\,321 - 123\,456\,789 = 864\,197\,532$
so, considering their digit sums, $45 - 45 = 45$.

104 Matchstick magic

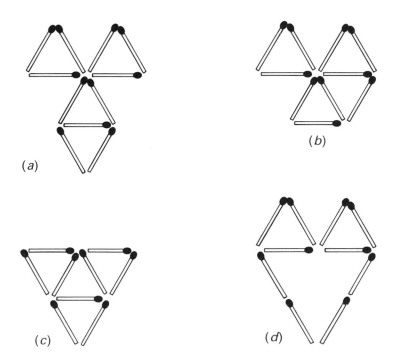

(a)

(b)

(c)

(d)

105 Two special square numbers

$1\,026\,753\,849 = 32\,043^2$
$9\,814\,072\,356 = 99\,066^2$

106 Locomotion!

There is no difference.

107 How numerate are you?

Here are a selection of possibilities, but many more are possible.

$$9 + 9 - 9 + \frac{9}{9} \qquad (9 + \frac{9}{9}) \times \frac{9}{9} \qquad 9 + \frac{9 + 9}{9 + 9}$$

$$9 + \frac{9 \times 9}{9 \times 9} \qquad 9 + \frac{\frac{9}{9}}{\frac{9}{9}} \qquad \frac{99}{9} - \frac{9}{9}$$

$$\frac{9}{0.9} + 9 - \sqrt{(9 \times 9)} \qquad \frac{9}{0.9} \times \frac{\sqrt{(9 \times 9)}}{9} \qquad 9\frac{9}{9} + \frac{9}{9}$$

$$\sqrt{9} + \sqrt{9} + \sqrt{9} + \frac{9}{9}$$

108 Reservoir revelations!

No, the answer is not a cube of side 20 m! It would have been if it was closed on the top, but for an open-top tank the most efficient design is to have a square horizontal cross-section, that is square in plan view, and the depth only half the width of the tank. In this case the tank would have approximate dimensions of:

$$25.2\,\text{m} \times 25.2\,\text{m} \times 12.6\,\text{m}$$

109 Domestic deliberations!

They have 300 pigs.

Let the number of pigs be n, and the number of available days of food be d. Then:

$$\frac{nd}{n - 75} = d + 20 \quad \text{and} \quad \frac{nd}{n + 100} = d - 15$$

$$20n - 75d = 1500 \qquad \text{and} \quad 15n - 100d = -1500$$

Solving simultaneously gives $n = 300$ and $d = 60$.

110 Target

The target of 329 can be achieved as follows:

$$(41 + 2) \times 7 + 28 = 329$$

To generate numbers to play the game with friends, or as a solitaire, a calculator could be used as follows. Let someone decide on a target number. Key the number into a calculator, then press the square root button an agreed number of times, say five. Then, starting from the left-hand end of the display, take the first two pairs of digits as two-digit numbers and the next three digits as single-digit numbers. For example, if the target number is 258, five presses of the square root key gives 1.1894964 and leads to the set (11, 89, 4, 9, 6) of numbers to be combined.

111 Back-packing!

The mule was carrying seven sacks of corn, and the donkey five. Suppose the mule carried x sacks and the donkey y sacks, then the mule's statements are equivalent to the equations:

$$x + 1 = 2(y - 1) \qquad x - 1 = y + 1$$

These can easily be solved simultaneously.

112 Multiple units!

Any number with an even number of digits always has 11 as a factor as can easily be inferred from the following sequence:

$$
\begin{aligned}
1111 &= 11 \times 101 \\
111111 &= 11 \times 10\,101 \\
11\,111\,111 &= 11 \times 1\,010\,101
\end{aligned}
$$

Further, any number with a multiple of three units digits will always have 3 and 37 as factors, for $111 = 3 \times 37$, and $111\,111 = 111 \times 1001$, $111\,111\,111 = 111 \times 1\,001\,001$, and so on. Hence all numbers of this form whose digit sum is even, or a multiple of three will factorise.

This only leaves for consideration those numbers whose digit sum is equal to a prime greater than 2 or 3 or a product of such primes. So far no easy way has been found to determine their factors, although

$$11\,111 = 41 \times 271$$
$$1\,111\,111 = 239 \times 4649$$
$$11\,111\,111\,111 = 21\,649 \times 513\,239$$
$$1\,111\,111\,111\,111 = 53 \times 79 \times 265\,371\,653$$
$$11\,111\,111\,111\,111\,111 = 2\,071\,723 \times 5\,363\,222\,357$$

At this point you may well be tempted to assume that all such numbers have factors. But what strange-looking factors they are, springing from such a unified starting point! Early this century the numbers consisting of 19 and 23 units digits were shown to be prime, after a considerable amount of effort. But no-one has yet found if the number with 47 units digits has any factors!

See *Recreations in the Theory of Numbers* by Albert Beiler (Dover) for further reading.

113   Dr Sharma's railway riddle

The wheels of railway rolling stock are coned, and the distance between the flanges of the two wheels allows some sideways movement on the rails. The result is that on a bend the outer wheel is riding on that part of the rim near the flange, giving it an effective radius which is larger than the radius of the wheel on the inside of the bend. By carefully designing the angle of the coning of the wheel rims and the allowable sideways movement, the slippage of the wheels is negligible.

Given that the rolling stock is designed so that the points of contact of a pair of wheels is 1.52 m apart, and that the sideways play allowed for is 8 mm, what should be the angle of coning for the wheel rims?

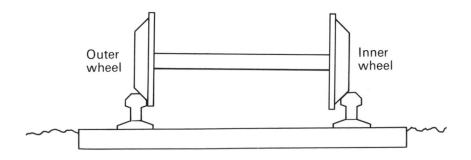

114 Batting exploits

Let the number of runs scored previously by the players be $2x$ and x respectively, and let n be the number of innings they had each had. Then:

$$\frac{2x + 33}{n + 1} = \frac{2x}{n} - 1 \qquad \frac{x + 33}{n + 1} = \frac{x}{n} + 1$$

from which, $n \neq 0$, multiplying by n and simplifying, we get:

$$n^2 + 34n = 2x \qquad 32n - n^2 = x$$

Eliminating x gives:

$$3n^2 - 30n = 0$$
$$3n(n - 10) = 0$$
$$n = 10$$

It follows that $x = 220$, and the batsmen's new averages are:

Slogger: 43   Missun: 23

115 How far to the lighthouse?

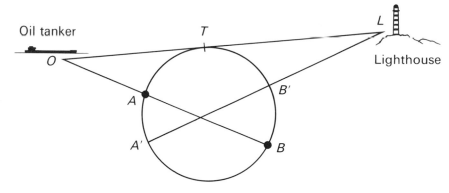

The lighthouse is 36 km away. Consider the result for a circle known as the tangent–secant theorem: $OT^2 = OA.OB$ (see diagram). If $OA = h$ metres is the height of an observer above sea level, and AB is the Earth's diameter in kilometres, then the distance d km from the observer to the horizon is given by:

$$d^2 = 0.001h(0.001h + 12\,800)$$

But as $0.001h$ is very small compared to $12\,800$, then for all practical purposes:

$$d^2 = 0.001h \times 12\,800 = 12.8h$$

Applying this twice – for the distances from the tanker and the lighthouse to the visible horizon – gives the required result.

112

116 How long is the ladder?

This is not as easy as it might first appear.

Let the length of each ladder be d, and let BM be x, (see the diagram). Then $VP = d - 3 = AP$, and $AM = 4 - x$.

Using Pythagoras' theorem:

$$AP^2 = AM^2 + MP^2$$
$$= AM^2 + PB^2 - MB^2, \text{ so}$$
$$(d - 3)^2 = (4 - x)^2 + 3^2 - x^2$$
$$d^2 - 6d - 16 + 8x = 0$$

But triangles PMB and VNB are similar, so:

$$\frac{x}{2} = \frac{3}{d}$$

giving:

$$x = \frac{6}{d}$$

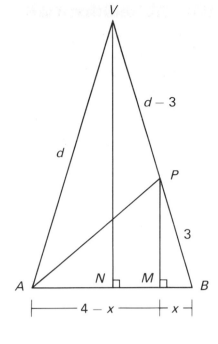

Substituting for x in the above equation leads to the cubic:

$$d^3 - 6d^2 - 16d + 48 = 0$$

Writing the left-hand side in the form:

$$f(d) = d[d(d - 6) - 16] + 48$$

enables $f(d)$ to be evaluated for different values of d and so gives $d = 7.2915$ m to 4 decimal places.

117 Convex pentagons are out!

Two solutions are shown with eight points, but I am led to believe that nine are possible. Help!

(a)

(b)

118 A healthy diet!

One solution is given here,
but it is not unique.

$$
\begin{array}{r}
45\,907 \\
+\ 40\,513 \\
\hline
86\,420
\end{array}
$$

119 A game to make you think!

Given any set of ten integers $n_1, n_2, \ldots n_{10}$, less than 100,
the number of possible subsets which can be chosen is
$2^{10} - 1 = 1023$. So the number of possible totals is 1023.
However, the largest possible total from ten integers less
than 100 is given by $90 + 91 + 92 + \ldots + 99 < 1000$.
Hence there are fewer than 1000 totals possible, so, with
1023 different subsets to choose from, their sums cannot all
be different. At least two will have the same total.

120 Nuptial flight!

There are 72 bees in the swarm.
   Let x be the number of bees in the swarm, then:

$$
x - \sqrt{\left(\frac{x}{2}\right)} - \frac{8x}{9} = 2
$$

from which:

$$
\frac{x}{9} - 2 = \sqrt{\left(\frac{x}{2}\right)}
$$

Squaring and simplifying leads to the quadratic equation:

$$
2x^2 - 153x + 648 = 0
$$

giving:

$$
(x - 72)(2x - 9) = 0
$$

and hence $x = 72$ is the only realistic solution.

121 Hexomino doubles!

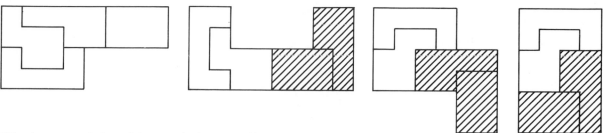

The key to solving this puzzle is to realise that of the twelve hexominoes given, eleven can be split into identical L shapes. So finding the four hexominoes which can be paired off into two Ls virtually solves the problem. The four required are shown, together with their solution. The first of these shapes is the odd one out, in that it does not split into two Ls like all the rest, but the same four hexominoes do fit together to make it. Having found how to make up the two Ls, they can often be fitted together in more than one way to provide a given shape, so the solution is not unique. The other eight shapes are shown as the combination of two Ls.

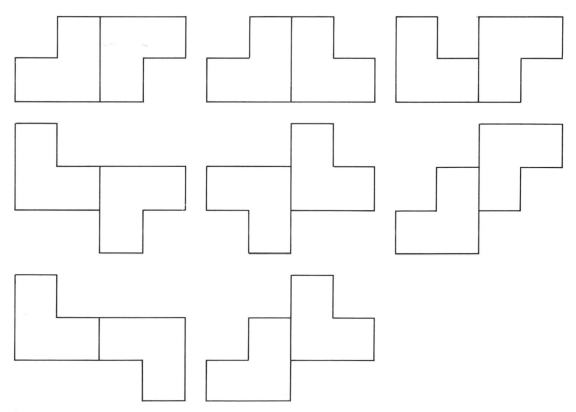

But you haven't finished yet! These four hexominoes will fit together to form yet three more different hexominoes. Which ones?

122 Coin cutting!

Only four coins need to be
removed, and the pattern is
unique apart from rotations
or reflections.

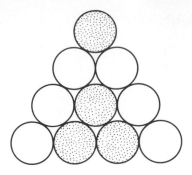

123 The photo cubes!

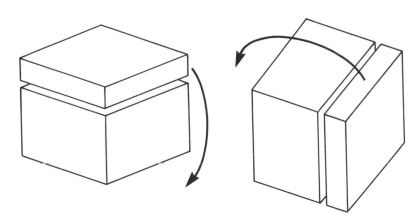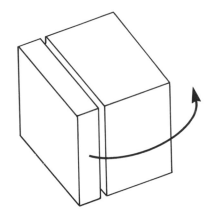

Consider the 4 × 4 × 4 cube after the first photos have been
stuck on and cut. First take the top layer of unit cubes and
move it to the bottom *en bloc*. This conceals the original
top and bottom photos between the two new bottom layers.
Next, take the front vertical layer and place it at the back.
This conceals the original front and back photos between
the new back layers. Then take the left-hand vertical layer
and place it at the right. This conceals the original left and
right photos between the new right-hand layers.

The cube can now have six new photos stuck on its faces
and cut into small squares.

The above process can now be repeated twice more and
six new photos stuck onto the untouched faces after each
rearrangement.

This process can easily be generalised to an $n \times n \times n$
cube if needed!

124   Non-intersecting knight's tours

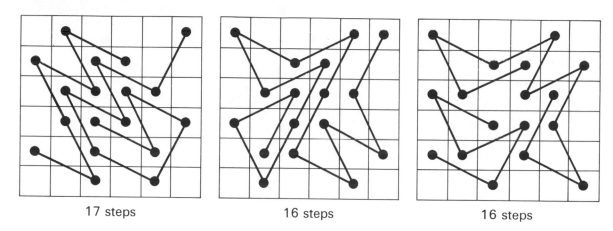

17 steps   16 steps   16 steps

The longest possible path contains 17 steps and is unique.
But don't be upset if you only achieved a path with 16, for
the originator of this type of puzzle, L. D. Yarborough,
believed that to be the optimum. There are in fact several
solutions of that length, although I spent some time before
finding any.

Now test your skill on 7×7 and 8×8 boards where the
optimum to aim for is 24 and 35 steps respectively.

125   Calculator challenge

$\frac{3363}{2378} = 1.4142136$ is accurate to 8 significant figures. See
activity 140 for a way of finding suitable numbers.

126   Rational cubes

$$\left(\frac{104\,940}{40\,831}\right)^3 + \left(\frac{11\,663}{40\,831}\right)^3 = 17$$

In essence, this is the problem of finding positive integers a,
b and c such that.

$$a^3 + b^3 = 17c^3$$

127 Coin squares

There are 21 squares in all:
  9 squares with sides of unit length;
  4 squares with sides of length $\sqrt{2}$;
  4 squares with sides of length $\sqrt{8}$;
  2 squares with sides of length $\sqrt{5}$;
  2 squares with sides of length $\sqrt{13}$.

It only requires the removal of six coins to ensure that no square of coins remains. For example, coins 3, 5, 6, 14, 15 and 20.

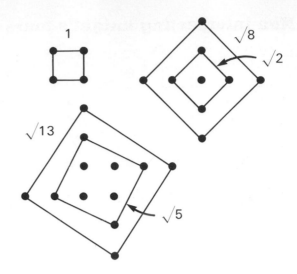

128 Cube rolling!

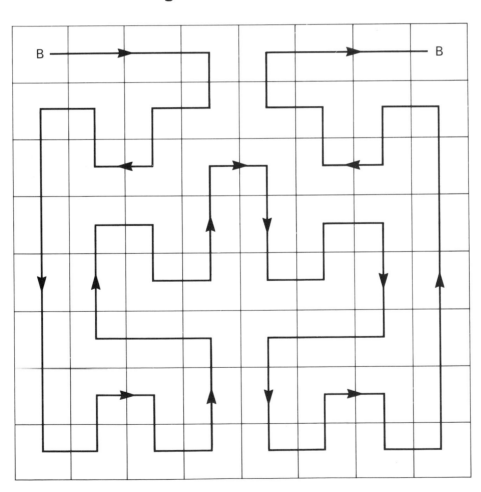

129 The random walk

This is based on one of Dudeney's early puzzles which he had in the context of a rook on a chessboard. Interestingly, the first solution he published was later shown not to be the optimum. He won't be the first or last setter of puzzles to have their solutions bettered!

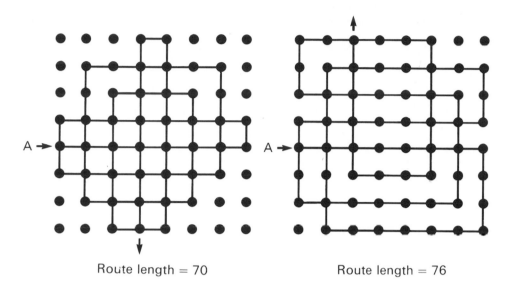

Route length = 70   Route length = 76

130 Net it!

The given net can only be filled in in one way, but there is more than one solution to a net where all the letters are standing upright. One is shown, together with its relation to the original net.

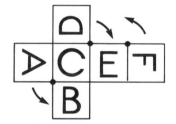
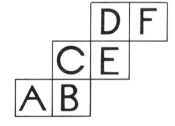

131 A Pythagorean prime property

The proof of this intriguing property is beyond the scope of this book, but a detailed account of this and similar properties may be found in *Recreations in the Theory of Numbers* by Albert Beiler (Dover).

132 Flattening a cube efficiently!

The eleven hexomino nets mentioned can be found in
Mathematical Activities by the author (Cambridge
University Press), activity 77. Three solutions are given
here, two attributable to John Costello. See his note in the
Mathematical Gazette, Vol. 75, No. 474, p. 436. The first
can be obtained by cutting both diagonals of the top face of
the cube and its four vertical edges, giving cuts of total
length $4 + 2\sqrt{2} \approx \mathbf{6.83}$ units.

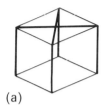

(a)

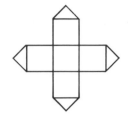

The second is similar. The diagonals of two opposite faces
are cut, together with an edge joining the faces, giving a
total length of $1 + 4\sqrt{2} \approx \mathbf{6.66}$ units.

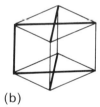

(b)

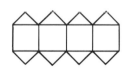

The third is quite ingenious and is based on Steiner's
shortest network to join four points at the vertices of a
square. By using this as a way of cutting two opposite faces
of the cube the net shown can be obtained requiring a total
length of cut of only $3 + 2\sqrt{3} \approx \mathbf{6.46}$ units.

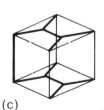

(c)

Steiner's network

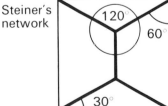

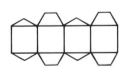

    Is it possible to do better?
    Note it should be clear that any solution will require a
cut to each corner of the cube.

133 Amicable numbers

The required numbers are 220 and 284.

Incidentally, 1184 and 1210 were discovered by a
16-year-old boy, B. N. I. Paganini, in 1866.

Other pairs are:

2620	2924
5020	5564
6232	6368

134 Rakesh at the cinema

A movie film is really a sequence of still photographs (the
frames) of a continuous motion, taken at $\frac{1}{16}$ second
intervals. When the resulting sequence is projected onto a
screen at the same time intervals we perceive the original
continuous motion because when we see anything our
minds retain the image a little longer than the actual time
spent looking at it. But how does this help to explain the
phenomenon observed by Rakesh?

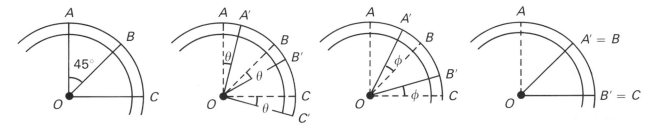

Suppose, for argument's sake, the stagecoach wheels have
eight equally spaced spokes. If the wheel is turning slowly
in a clockwise direction, then in the $\frac{1}{16}$ second time interval
between successive frames the spokes will have turned
through a small angle θ, OA will have advanced to OA', OB
to OB'. The mind interprets this as a clockwise rotation. As
the speed of rotation increases the angle θ increases from
one frame to the next. Of course, the eye cannot distinguish
one spoke from another, and when θ becomes greater than
22.5°, instead of seeing the new position of OA as a
clockwise rotation of θ, it interprets the new position as an
anticlockwise rotation of $\phi = 45° - \theta$ from the previous
position of OB, as this is closer. As the speed of rotation
increases, ϕ becomes smaller so the wheel will appear to the
observer to be slowing down while still rotating the wrong
way. A further increase in speed will bring OA' to coincide
with OB, and the effect is that the wheel appears to become
stationary.

The idea for this item came from Professor Roger
Eggleton from the University of Brunei Darussalam.

135 The vertical drop!

The food parcels all leave the
plane with the same forward
speed as the plane, so
although gravity is
accelerating them downwards
their forward speed remains
the same as that of the plane.
Therefore to a distant
observer, seeing them against
the background of the sky,
they will appear to be falling
in a vertical line beneath the
plane. But their trajectories
all approximate to parabolas
(see the diagram) which strike
the ground at different points.
This explanation ignores the
effect of air resistance, a
reasonable assumption, as a
food parcel is a dense object.

In contrast, paratroopers
leaving a plane appear to
drop vertically until they
open their parachutes, when
the effect of air resistance is
very significant.

137 The home stretch!

Various solutions are considered here, each an improvement
on its predecessor. In each case the unit of length is taken
as the edge of the cube.

1   First consider a web which follows the edges of the box.
    To connect all eight corners it will require a minimum
    of seven edges. *AEHDCGFB* is such a web with a length
    of **7** units.

2   Another possibility is to have a web consisting of the
    four long diagonals of the box. This has a length of
    $4 \times \sqrt{3} \approx$ **6.928** units.

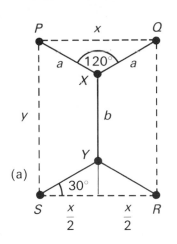

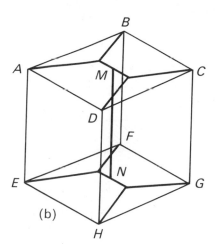

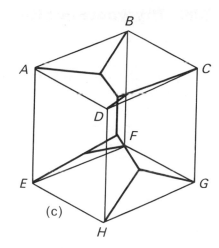

To improve on these, appeal is made to Steiner's minimum network for four points at the vertices of a rectangle (see diagram (a)), where all the angles at X and Y are 120°. If the rectangle is x units by y units, then simple trigonometry gives $a = x/\sqrt{3}$, $b = y - x/\sqrt{3}$, and the network joining P, Q, R and S has a total length of $4a + b = y + x\sqrt{3}$.

3   $ABCD$ and $EFGH$, see diagram (b), are each joined by a Steiner network of length $1 + \sqrt{3}$ ($x = 1$, $y = 1$), and the middle of each network is joined to the other by a strand of web, MN of length 1, giving a web of total length $3 + 2\sqrt{3} \approx$ **6.464** units.

4   Now consider a web consisting of two Steiner networks joining $ABGH$ and $DCFE$. They meet in the middle of the box so need no joining link. In this case $x = 1$ and $y = \sqrt{2}$ for each network, giving a web of total length $2(\sqrt{2} + \sqrt{3}) \approx$ **6.292** units.

5   Can this solution be improved on? Well yes! Consider again the solution depicted in diagram (b). Imagine the Y-pieces of the Steiner networks on each side of M and N drawn towards the centre of the cube, keeping all the angles of the Ys at 120°, but stretching their trunks, until MN is at 120° to each of the Y's trunks – see diagram (c). A straightforward application of trigonometry gives the resulting web a total length of $1 + 3\sqrt{3} \approx$ **6.196** units.

    This last solution was suggested to me by John Costello of Loughborough University.

Now try your hand with the equivalent problem for the six vertices of a regular octahedron.

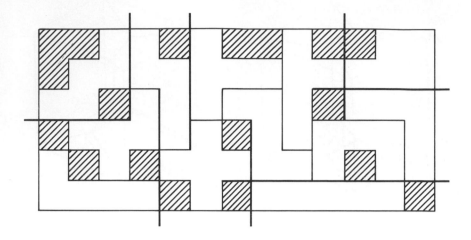

Here is a solution. The heavy lines indicate the first cuts to be made, and careful thought will enable you to see how further straight cuts can then be made which will produce all the pentominoes apart from the U shape. Try cutting it out with a pair of scissors from a paper plan if you cannot visualise all the required cuts. Solutions have been found for a 4 × 19 rectangle with area 76 square units and, even better, for a 5 × 15 rectangle with area 75 square units. But it is not yet known if this is the smallest rectangle for which a solution is possible. Over to you.

This and many other polyomino puzzles are to be found in the book *Polyominoes* by Solomon W. Golomb (George Allen and Unwin).

141 Artificial gravity

The floor would be on the outside edge of the tube with people walking so that their heads pointed towards the centre of the wheel. If the wheel is rotated at such a speed that $r\omega^2 = g$, where r is the radius of the outside of the tube and ω its angular velocity, then the people will experience their normal weight as they walk around in the tube. You might think that they would be forever walking uphill as the floor will always appear to curve upwards in front of them, but as they walk around the rim of the wheel the force they experience between their feet and the floor will always point towards the wheel's centre, so it will feel as if they are walking on the level.

If the spokes of the wheel communicate with a laboratory at the hub, then the people would experience weightlessness in the laboratory, and would need a lift to carry them along a communicating spoke! Think about it!

142 Taking Mansfield for a walk

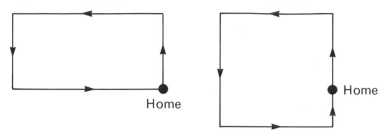

With the first set of constraints a walk can end after four
legs, with the last leg at right angles to the first, or after five
legs with the last leg in the same direction as the first. The
first leg can be 1, 2, 3, . . . or 8 blocks long, and for each of
these the second leg can also be from 1 to 8 blocks long.
Hence the number of possible walks is:

$$1 \times 8 + 2 \times 8 + 3 \times 8 + \ldots + 8 \times 8 = 288$$

As 1988 was a leap year (so February had 29 days), they
completed their walks on 14 October 1988.

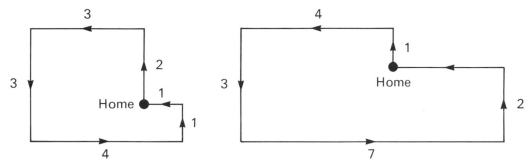

Dr Fit's second set of constraints introduces all the
L-shaped walks like those shown with six legs. There are a
surprising number of these. Consider all such routes where
the first two legs are of length 1 block. The third and fourth
legs could be any length from 2 to 8, giving 7×7 walks.
Keeping the first leg at 1 block, and increasing the second
leg to 2 blocks, still leaves the third leg with 7 possible
lengths, but reduces the fourth leg to a choice from 3 to 8
blocks, giving 7×6 further walks. By systematically
increasing the second leg from 1 to 7, it can be seen that
the number of walks with the first leg 1 block long is given
by:

$$7(1 + 2 + 3 + 4 + 5 + 6 + 7)$$

In a similar way, we need to consider what happens when
the first leg is of length 2. This leads to:

$$6(1 + 2 + 3 + 4 + 5 + 6 + 7)$$

further walks.

Similarly, by considering the possible walks when the first leg is of length 3, 4, 5, 6, 7 we find that the total number of L-shaped walks is:

$$(1 + 2 + 3 + 4 + 5 + 6 + 7)(1 + 2 + 3 + 4 + 5 + 6 + 7) = 28^2,$$

so together with the original 288 rectangular walks this gives a grand total of 1072 different walks.

Now there were 366 days in 1988 and 365 days in each of 1989 and 1990, a total of 1096, 24 more than the number of walks, so Mansfield received his new collar on 7 December 1990.

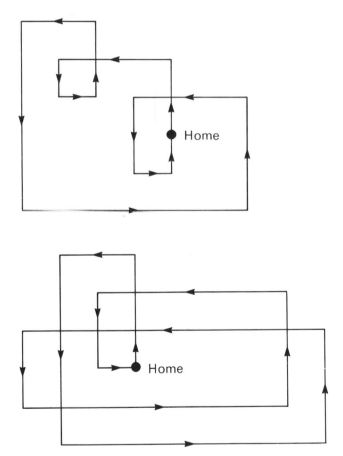

As for Dr Fit's third set of walks, he could never live long enough to enjoy the great variety he had unleashed! Just consider the two examples shown to appreciate the very large number of possible routes, and their complexity. The question this still leaves unanswered, though, is how many such routes are there?

A good note on which to end this book!

The main ideas for this item came from Professor Roger Eggleton, from the University of Brunei Darussalam.